CAR

SECRETS

REVEALED

by

Corey Rudl

Published by: Car Secrets   U.S. Address: Car Secrets
               RR#2, 11 Doe Road   812 Proctor Avenue
               Carleton Place, ON   Ogdensburg, NY
               K7C 3P2   13669

Special thanks to Hope Rudl and Ron Speck
Edited by: Chris Lennon, Jeff Puthuff

First Edition: April 1995
Second Edition: March 1996
Third Edition: November 1996

PRINTED IN THE UNITED STATES

IMPORTANT

READ THIS FIRST!

Dear Friend,

Your decision to purchase this book may turn out to be one of the smartest moves you've ever made. This book is designed to be an advocate for consumers who must deal with an industry that can often be characterized as based on greed. Therefore, some readers may misinterpret my approach as negative. Nothing could be further from the truth. Many segments of the industry are self-policing, and still others are reinventing themselves so that they can service existing customers better and attract new ones.

This book delivers completely on every promise I've made in my advertising. Every money saving idea you are about to read has already been tested and is proven to work. These ideas have <u>already</u> saved vast amounts of money and put those savings directly back into the pockets of the very select group of people that I have shared this information with in the past.

An extremely important point must first be made. It doesn't matter if you are only interested in certain sections,

READ EVERY SECTION OF THIS BOOK
FROM COVER TO COVER!

Yes, **this means you! There will be many, and I mean <u>many</u>, tips and hints in every section that apply to everyone.** For example, if you are interested in finding the best service center for your car, you may only want to read Chapter 1. However, there are other valuable tips throughout the rest of the book that relate to this.

Similarly, even if you are not in the market for a new vehicle, you should read the section entitled "Buying Your New Car" — it is really fascinating. You'll learn about all the tricks behind "too good to be true" advertising and sales gimmicks, and I'll show you how to test the dealership's service center.

This is done because when you are buying a new car, your greatest concern should <u>not</u> be the price — I can show you how to get the same great deal anywhere. However, you should be concerned about the way the service center treats you and their policies on warranty work. Although this may not seem important right now, it will become very clear as you read through the chapters and find out what <u>really</u> goes on behind those service center doors and the polite service reps, whether you are buying a new car or not.

Somewhere along the line you are sure to start wondering why I am revealing all of these inside tips and secrets. I hear stories every day about people who think they were swindled, but don't know for sure. All they know is that their repair bill seemed awfully high, without knowing why or what to do about it. I wanted to show people how a vast amount of our automobile expense could be reduced drastically (save 30% on gas, reduce insurance by 50%, how to buy the right car cheap, etc.). People could get this information elsewhere, but at an outrageous cost. For example, a report similar to mine, *How to Drive a Luxury Car Free Every Year*, was sold by a Florida man for $495, when it cost a mere few dollars to print. It disturbs me to see the consumer being blind-sided, and I felt it was time for someone to be on your side.

When I write, it is in a no-nonsense, straight forward and sometimes highly enthusiastic manner. I don't have a Ph.D. in English (which I've heard really means Piled Higher and Deeper), so if it's a literary style you are looking for — you may find my writing annoying, confusing and a bit out of the ordinary. However, if information is what you want...this is the book for you.

I have spent more than seven years researching all the secrets found in this book. I have owned two specialty car companies since the age of 17, talked with over 100 manufacturers, suppliers and experts, and consulted with literally thousands of car enthusiasts. **All of this knowledge is now yours, and all you have to do is read on!**

Happy Motoring!

Corey Rudl
Former President, Prestige Auto

P.S. You will benefit more if you read this book from beginning to end instead of 'hopping around' from one section to another. Some chapters may seem boring if you are not interested in a particular subject, but there are a few tidbits of information in each section that you will find amazing even if you skim through to sections that are of more interest to you.

TABLE OF CONTENTS

REDUCE YOUR INSURANCE BY UP TO 50%

Reducing your insurance is easier than you probably imagine. There are a multitude of ways to reduce your rates. You should choose the ones that apply to you and then take this information to your local insurance company.

The average person spends hundreds, if not thousands of dollars a year on insurance. Up to 50% of this can be avoided. The idea is to get adequate coverage at minimal costs.

Premiums are influenced by a few factors: the value of your vehicle, your driving record, where you live, your marital status, age, sex, and the model of car you drive.

If you own a cottage, register the car to that address. You will get a much better rate if you are in the country where accidents are less common than in the city.

If you are under 25 (especially if you're male) and have parents that can register and insure the car under their name with you as the principle driver, do so. It is even better if they live in suburban or rural areas where rates are lower.

If you have a teenage driver at home, restrict his/her use of the car to less than 25% so he/she is listed as an occasional driver. If they were stated as a principle driver, the insurance cost could almost double!

Also, if you have your own business, having your teenager use a company car will save the most in insurance premiums. Most insurance companies do not increase premiums on company cars for teenage drivers.

The following coverage is generally a waste of money: emergency towing service coverage (especially if it is covered by your auto club), car rental expense coverage, and duplicate medical coverage already covered by a health or insurance plan (usually from your place of employment). You generally pay much more for these services. To eliminate them, just call your broker and explain what you want removed from your policy.

Increase the deductible on your car to the highest level. You can pay ridiculous rates for a $50 deductible compared to $500. This could reduce your insurance from 20%-40%. It just makes sense. Remember the deductible is only paid if the collision is your fault, not the other party's. So what are the chances of you causing an accident? Anyway, you generally don't want to claim anything under $500 because your insurance rates will increase, depending on how many claims you have made.

Remember when buying a car, the bigger the engine, the more the insurance. Don't be too quick to put more horsepower in the car than you need. You may find yourself paying a large price for this pleasure when it comes to insuring the vehicle.

Studies show certain cars are most susceptible to theft or accidents. These cars have surcharges applied to them. This only applies to the collision and comprehensive portion of your insurance, and only amounts to about a 10% increase at the most. A listing of the rate of theft and accidents (including deaths) for every car manufactured is made available in a free brochure from The Institute for Highway Safety, 1005 North Glebe Road, Arlington, VA 22201.

If an accident has forced you into a high-risk category, a leasing company (if you are leasing a car) may provide insurance coverage for much less.

One of the heaviest premiums is on business use or travel to work. If you don't use your car for these, activities <u>make</u> <u>sure</u> the insurance company knows that. It could save you a lot of money. If you are a two car family, try to use one for work and the other for occasional driving.

IF YOUR CAR IS NOT WORTH $3,000
IT USUALLY DOES NOT PAY TO HAVE COLLISION COVERAGE

The risk to reward ratio is too low to warrant it. Remember, collision insurance only covers you for repairs to your car if you hit someone. If someone hits you, their insurance pays for your repair, including car rental, towing, etc. If you hit someone and have regular liability insurance (required by law in most states) but don't have collision coverage, your insurance company will <u>still</u> pay for the repair for the car you hit, but not the repairs to your car.

I will also show you a way to open your own home-based business in the next section so that...

ALL YOUR INSURANCE PREMIUMS
BECOME TAX DEDUCTIBLE!

You can purchase a limited mileage plan. Many companies understand that you may only drive your car occasionally. They have developed plans where you pay <u>much</u> less for the policy, but are limited to a certain number of miles per year.

When you visit your insurance company, don't forget to ask for any discounts that apply to you! There are existing discounts for:

1) senior citizens
2) alarm systems
3) driver training courses
4) good driving record
5) students with a higher than "B" average (there actually is!)
6) college student away from home without car
7) safety devices (like air bags and anti-lock brakes)
8) nonsmoker or nondrinker
9) participation in car pool
10) car use for pleasure only
11) multiple vehicles covered under the same policy
12) multiple policies (auto, boat, home, life insurance)

For example, Allstate offers a 15% discount if all your policies are with their company, or if you have more than one car on your policy.

Discounts for safety features can be very large with specific companies. For example, USAA offers a 60% discount on medical and personal injury insurance for cars with airbags. Nationwide offers a 50% discount for air bags which protect both the driver and passenger, a 40% discount for driver-side airbag, and 20% discounts for automatic seat belts. Allstate and USAA also offer discounts on collision and liability premiums (10% and 5%, respectively) for vehicles with four wheel anti-lock brakes.

ONE INSURANCE COMPANY MAY CHARGE YOU <u>DOUBLE</u> WHAT ANOTHER CHARGES FOR IDENTICAL COVERAGE!

Don't be afraid to shop around for prices. Company rates can vary <u>drastically</u>. It may save you a lot of money. Let your regular insurance company know that you are shopping around. They may be more flexible with your rates, especially if you already have policies with them.

As a last resort, you may want to consider buying insurance from a mail order insurance company, but check their background and make sure they are legitimate. It is usually cheaper than your local insurance agent.

As a final note, most auto insurance policies transfer over to a rental car automatically if it is rented in your name. Before you waste $7-15/day in rental insurance, call your agent to see if this applies to your policy.

HOW TO PAY THOUSANDS LESS IN TAXES (LEGALLY) BY LISTING YOUR CAR INTEREST ON YOUR TAX RETURN

The difference between tax evasion and tax avoidance should be made clear. Tax evasion involves the illegal denial and concealment of an existing tax liability — like unreported income sources, etc. Tax avoidance is planning so you prevent a tax liability from coming into existence and perfectly legal. This may be done by the way a transaction or business is organized, or by a selection of options in the tax laws.

One common method of paying less tax is called the "shift". This is where you may not have enough of an itemized deduction to qualify for the minimum standard amount. You hold that deduction until the next fiscal year, and add it to that year's deductions; thereby qualifying and taking advantage of those deductions.

To maximize your tax advantage, you can establish one of two approaches: the investment, or the business approach. The key to either method is the intent to make a profit. Your investment or business must be making a profit.

Do not get discouraged,

ESTABLISHING THE INTENT TO MAKE A PROFIT IN BUSINESS OR INVESTMENT IS EASILY DONE

The IRS knows very well that in the first few years of a business it is common to operate at a substantial loss and make large write-offs. However, if you consistently lose money over a period of years, the IRS can accuse you of operating a hobby as a business and can disallow the deductions. To build evidence in your favor, you might want to consider doing the following things: participate in car shows, car auctions, automobile clubs, generate promotions with your automobile (if it is an exotic or classic car unless you are using public transportation to and from work). It is also very good to prepare a business or investment budget.

Let's first look at the **investment approach**. This is perfect for antique, classic, exotic cars, specialty cars, street rods and restorations. This approach is your best option if your automobile transactions are performed only once or a few times a year.

The idea behind the investment approach is that you want to maintain your car in the expectation (not requirement) that the asset will appreciate in value and you will sell your vehicle for profit. Examples of some of the expenses you can deduct on your tax return are:

1. General maintenance and repair
2. Insurance
3. Telephone calls
4. Storage expense, including the portion of the building's depreciation, maintenance, insurance and utilities
5. Travel expenses, including lodging and meals for any matter that regards taking care of your investment. (This does not include travel expense for investigating a new automobile as an investment)
6. Wages of a secretary (maybe your wife or children) or for bookkeeping

You cannot deduct a portion of your house as office space because you are not running a business. This scenario is the same as if you were investing in stocks, but the stocks are your car.

Also be aware that any large expense for the improvement of the investment vehicle is not considered an expense and written-off. It is added to the asset's (car's) value in your books. When you sell your car, whether in 1 month or 3 years, you will claim the gain or loss of your entire investment vehicle (including the large improvement expense) at that point.

It is important that this is not your only car. The IRS must be convinced that it is only taken on the occasional trip for a rod run or car show, to the repair shop, a parade, etc. To establish this, you may want to obtain a special insurance policy that has mileage limits on it (and much lower rates).

The **business approach** is a little different. The concept behind this approach is that you are in the business of buying, possessing and reselling automobiles for profit. You can even obtain income from prize money (car show), and special services rendered like consulting. This is perfect for someone who changes cars frequently (especially sports cars), or is restoring vehicles within a year. It can be formed as a sole proprietorship, partnership, or corporation. However, a sole proprietorship is the easiest of all.

What does it take to start your own business? **It is very easy.** Most states require you to fill out a form declaring your business name and address to obtain a business license.

Open a checking account in the business's name, and use that account for business purposes only. It is also necessary to get business cards, letterhead, and invoices printed up. This can be done at a local stationary store for a small fee, or on any personal computer.

If you are concerned about buying and selling cars to be eligible to make tax deductions, I have great news for you. In a book that I am just finishing right now (it should be available by May 1996), I can show you how to make huge profits from home being an automotive agent without ever buying a car or even using or risking one cent of your money, by simply making some phone calls every few days. Hundreds of people are using the technique I reveal in my new book and are making a killing! It is simple, easy, and involves so little time, that it is pure ingenuity. If you are interested, request information on this book from the publisher (address on copyright page).

Examples of deductions you can make with the business approach are as follows:

1. Depreciation of the automobile(s), tow trailers, machinery or any major piece of office equipment (including computers and fax machines)

2. Bank service charges, business licensing, and accountant fees
3. Storage, including the building's depreciation, maintenance, insurance and utility costs
4. Travel expenses, including lodging and meals for any show, meets, or prospects of buying another car (only 50-80% of meals are allowed for deduction)
5. Business portion of home, including mortgage payments or rent, mortgage interest, utilities, etc.
6. Office equipment and supplies
7. Wages for employees (wife and children perhaps) who maintain books or work on vehicles
8. Advertising and promotions
9. Repairs and maintenance to car(s)
10. Club fees, business registration fees, etc.
11. Telephone expenses
12. Automotive magazines or training materials

You can even deduct transportation from your shop (possibly your garage) to pick up automotive parts in town. These include depreciation, insurance, gas, repairs, parking fees, etc. However, an easier way is to use the government's standard mileage rate of 27.5 cents a mile (current for 1994 year). The expense is taken by calculating all the business miles put on the car and multiplying that by the standard mileage rate for that year.

Since this book is training material for your business...YOU CAN ALSO DEDUCT THE PRICE OF THIS BOOK ON YOUR NEXT TAX RETURN IF YOU ADOPT THE BUSINESS APPROACH.

Also, if you trade a car for another vehicle, and it is an even trade, **it is tax-free.** If you exchange your vehicle (plus $5,000 cash) for another vehicle, the $5,000 will be the portion of the car that is taxable. Contact your local DMV for the proper paperwork. The transaction should be classified as an exchange, not a sale.

If you operate your business as a sole proprietorship, you can claim your profit or loss on schedule C of your tax return. If you have a net profit over $400, you must also file a schedule SE. Don't worry, these forms are straight forward and easy to understand.

In the business approach, you must claim all expenses incurred in that current year. However, the investment approach offers one great benefit. Let's say you do not exceed the standard deduction for the year on your current tax return for an itemized deduction. You are allowed to hold-over that deduction and let it accumulate until the car is sold and claim it then.

Since tax laws change every year and the paper work can be sometimes tiresome, you should hire a local tax accountant to do the actual form filing. As long as you know the principles behind what you are trying to do, let the tax accountant do the work of figuring out where the numbers go, and on what form. He's a professional and does this everyday. He can do it many times faster that you, and in my opinion, it is usually worth every penny.

MANY PEOPLE ASK ME "WHAT ARE THE CHANCES OF BEING AUDITED?"

Even though this is completely legal and you have a right to take advantage of the techniques here, some of my clients have been concerned that it will trigger "red flags" at the IRS office and they will be audited.

As we all know, an audit can be a real hassle.

These techniques will not set up any "red flags", or draw any attention to you. Millions of people are using these types of techniques every year on their tax return.

About 1.5% of all returns are audited. If you are earning $50,000 a year or more, the rate jumps to 8% — four times the average. However if you are earning less than $25,000, it drops to about 0.6%. So don't be paranoid. And even if you did get audited, you have nothing to hide. If you have done everything legally, don't worry. Stories of a cruel and ruthless IRS are blown way out of proportion.

If you presently own your own business in some other area of interest (i.e. computer store, craft making, etc.), you may already know some of the tax advantages when using your automobile for business. You can write-off any expense incurred for business use (gas, maintenance, insurance, etc.) and even write-off a portion of the depreciation over the year. This depreciation alone can add hundreds of dollars to your tax refund each year.

Lastly, remember tax laws change every year, so make sure you update yourself on any changes that may affect you before proceeding with any methods explained in this chapter.

I will show you three ways to save 20 - 40% on any part you need for repairs. This section alone will save you hundreds, if not thousands, of dollars.

Before we get into that, let's discuss the quality of auto parts. Are in-house brand names for retail chain stores as good as parts from GM, Ford, Honda, or any of the manufacturers?

The answer, surprisingly, is that...

MANY OF THESE PARTS ARE THE SAME, JUST IN DIFFERENT BOXES.

For example, a parts manufacturer that makes starters will have starters coming off the assembly line; some of which will go in GM boxes, some in Wagner boxes, some in Sears boxes, etc. They are all the same starter!

You may buy a Toyota car that has an air filter with the Toyota name on it, but in fact it is built by Fram. You'll never know the difference until you price them. The Toyota filter will be much more expensive.

The only difference most of between these duplicate parts are the price and warranty. The car manufacturer OEM part (like GM, Toyota, Chrysler, etc.) will most likely have the highest price, followed by the aftermarket supplier (like Wagner, Fram, etc.). The lowest price will be the no-name brand that goes into K-Mart, Midas, UAP (United Auto Parts) etc. The warranty will be longest for OEM parts, then for aftermarket followed by no-name. Sometimes the differences are very significant. For example, a GM warranty may be 24 months/30,000 miles, when the no-name warranty on the same part may be 30 days/1,000 miles. Make sure you are aware of the differences.

Not all parts are from quality manufacturers, but many main components are. Consider buying any major replacement items from a "house" brand like Canadian Tire, UAP, NAP, etc. This is one way to save big money on parts. Their starters, batteries, air filters, alternators, brake pads, etc. are generally made by a quality manufacturer. Brand name parts will usually be 40 - 100% more expensive. If you are concerned about the warranty, or if you want high-performance parts, then you may want to spend the money for brand names. I'll show you how to save 20-40% off even these parts.

I'll be speaking about auto parts stores and suppliers in this section. Don't get them confused. When I talk about an auto parts store, I am referring to the ones just like your local NAPA store, speed shop, or the equivalent; places where you can get replacement parts for your vehicle. When I speak of suppliers, I am referring to specialty businesses that are usually not locally owned and operated. They can be found throughout the country and specialize in some particular area of the auto parts industry. These suppliers mainly offer their product via mail-order. If you spend a total of $1500 in parts per year, a 40% saving means...

YOU CAN SAVE UP TO $600 IMMEDIATELY!

There are four main categories in the automotive price structure: wholesale, jobber, dealer (or garage), and retail. Wholesale is the price at which a manufacturer of a product sells to a distributor, usually about 30% above cost. This distributor may carry hundreds of manufacturer's product lines. This allows the distributor to offer hundreds and even thousands of products to a retail store. That way, a retail auto parts store only has to deal with one or two distributors. The retail stores buy from the distributors at "jobber" pricing (an auto parts store is considered a jobber), which includes about a 25% mark-up over what the distributor paid. They sell at retail price which has an additional 35% mark-up.

Have I missed the dealer category? Not really. This is the price a mechanic's garage (or repair shop) will purchase at, right between jobber and retail pricing. The garage will then in turn charge the consumer full retail price.

If you haven't followed this, go back and read it over until you understand it completely. It is vital that you understand this principle.

The car dealership has basically three price categories: their cost, garage price (approx. 20% markup), and retail (approx. 40% markup over cost).

It is important to understand mark-up. Read the following carefully, since it can be confusing. If I have a product that costs me $120 and I want 30% mark-up, I take 100% and subtract 30% to get an answer of 70%. As you know, 70% is 0.7 in decimal (move the decimal two places to the left). I then divide my cost price of $120 by 0.7 which equals $171.43. The price with 30% mark-up is $171.43. If you don't understand this, get your calculator and follow it through.

Whoa...I must be crazy, right? $120 multiplied by 30% is $156 not $171.43. You are absolutely correct. That is why mark-up is so tricky and you have to understand the concept. The 30% mark-up is the percentage amount that I can subtract from my selling price to get my cost price. It is not just multiplying my cost price by 30%,...

IT IS ACTUALLY MULTIPLYING MY COST PRICE BY 43%!

Confusing, huh? If you don't understand this, try thinking about it this way. Take a $100 product and add 30% to get a selling price of $130. If you take that selling price of $130 and subtract 30% thinking you are going to end up with your cost price, you are wrong — $130 subtract 30% equals $91, not $100.

Now that you understand that, recall that the price mark-up difference between the auto parts store cost price and its retail price is about 35%. In other words, they multiply their cost price by 1.54 which is a 50% increase in price, but only a 35% mark-up.

I will explain the simplest and easiest way to get 20% off every part you buy from the auto parts store. As explained above, auto parts stores work on very large profit margins. You can use this to your advantage.

SIMPLY APPROACH THE OWNER OF
YOUR LOCAL AUTO PARTS STORE
AND STATE YOUR SITUATION!

Many of them will give you garage price if you do a lot of business with them. This is extremely effective with a "mom and pop" auto parts store. It may be more difficult with an auto parts chain stores (unless you know the owner).

The scenario may go something like this: "Hi, Mr. Owner, my name is John Doe. I am presently purchasing a lot of parts for repairs to my 1987 Corvette convertible. I probably buy at least $2,000 worth of parts and accessories a year. I have been going from store to store trying to find the best price for each of the parts I need. This is starting to become tiresome and aggravating. I would like to make you a proposition I think will benefit both of us. If you will give me dealer price on everything I purchase, I will keep all of my business here and not bother to shop around. That would mean a <u>bonus</u> of at least $2,000 in sales that you weren't expecting. What do you think"?

This is even more so if you are buying a quantity of parts over a short period of time; as in restoring or fixing up an older car.

You may even want to up the yearly expenditure figure because you might be able to start buying parts for your friends and neighbors at this rate and charge them your cost or add 5% to 10% for your time and hassle. Either way, you will entice the store owner to give you a deal because you will have a higher yearly expenditure and you will make a few bucks on the side (you can use this as your home-based business mentioned in the previous chapter, if you wish). If you decide to sell parts to your friends, do not let the owner know this. It can cause hard feelings, since he probably would have sold the part at full retail to them.

This can not be done with all auto parts stores. Most large franchises have strict pricing policies in their franchise agreement, and cannot break them without accepting the possible consequences with the franchiser. However, if these stores are owner-operated, you will find that many of them will bend the rules if you talk to the owner personally. It can't hurt to ask. As a rule, almost any small operation that is owner-operated will agree to your terms.

If your offer to an auto parts store you really would like to deal with gets rejected, there is a very powerful closing statement that may sway their decision. "No, you say? I am surprised. My next stop is your competitor. I can't believe you would give this business to them on a silver platter. Would you rather have your competition making the extra $2,000 a year instead of you"?

Some speed shops and auto parts stores have a machine shop built in to the operation. If you decided to negotiate a deal with one of these shops, make sure the dealer price includes discounts at the machine shop as well, since you might have to use them again.

If you decide you would like to sell some parts to your friends for a little profit, you should start a business from your home that sells auto parts and accessories. There is a little paperwork involved, and it will take some of your time, but you now not only save money on your purchases and make a few bucks from your friends, but most importantly...

**YOU QUALIFY FOR ALL THE TAX DEDUCTIONS
A BUSINESS IS ALLOWED.
THE MONEY SAVED ON YOUR TAX RETURN
CAN BE HUNDREDS, IF NOT THOUSANDS
OF DOLLARS A YEAR.**

By having a business license, you **automatically** get dealer pricing on any part in any auto parts store. I will even show you how to get 40% off using this method later on in this section.

Another benefit of this method is that you can purchase any part from a car dealership and get garage pricing on OEM parts. This can save you big bucks because their prices are so high. Let me illustrate. I wanted to buy four Cavalier Z24 wheel caps (retail price $44.10 each). I stated that I was from Prestige Auto and asked what is the garage price? "About $27" was the reply. It's that easy.

I SAVED $68.34 ON A $176.40 PURCHASE!

That's right, it only cost me $108.06 for the parts, plus I have a choice of paying sales tax. If the car is on the inventory of my company, I can add the cost of the caps to the book value. Therefore, the sales tax will be paid by the guy who buys my car. The other option is to pay the sales tax because you are not reselling the item, then write the entire expense off in your books as car maintenance. If you are confused, the next few paragraphs about another business venture should clear things up.

Many people who hire my consulting services say, "It's great that I save 20% on parts, but how can I do that when I am at a large auto chain store getting my car fixed"?

There are three plans of action you can take. The first is to mark on your repair order that you want a quote for parts, but none installed without your authorization. When the service technician tells you what parts you will need, either pick these up at the auto parts store you have a "deal" with, or tell the technician to order the parts from that store because you get special pricing.

The second approach is to speak to the service manager. Politely state that you can get a special price from ABC auto parts store and you can buy these parts there if they wish. State that you like his service center and would prefer to do business with them (as not to create bad feelings) if they can match the discount the ABC parts store is giving you. If they refuse, just buy your parts at ABC and have them delivered to where your car is being repaired. However, most of the time the service manager will take the business, even though he is not making as much money as he would like. Some profit is better than no profit.

The third approach is opening a company as mentioned previously. You would just state, "I am from ABC Auto Enterprises. Please do a quote with all dealer pricing before you start the repairs". It's that easy.

If you decided to open a business and use the "business approach" as mentioned in the "Save $1,000s on Your Taxes" section, everything you purchase can be tax-exempt. Remember, that this is for your display car which is up for resale when it is complete (recall that anything bought for resale or to assemble into resalable products is tax exempt). But remember, if you keep the car for yourself and close your business, then you will be responsible for the taxes that were exempted.

The main advantage to this, compared to negotiating a deal with the store owner, is that you can get dealer pricing anywhere at anytime **and** you will be tax exempt for the parts you buy.

The third and last way to get discounts on your parts is the finest of them all.

YOU WILL GET 30% TO 40% OFF
EVERY PART YOU PURCHASE!

You will need to have your own business, as mentioned above. Since you own a business that can legally purchase parts and sell them at a retail level, you are <u>entitled</u> to deal with the distributors directly instead of purchasing them through the auto parts store. You will be buying the parts for the same price the auto parts stores do — at <u>jobber</u> pricing.

The distributor will require a business address, a copy of your business and tax licenses, and shipping instructions (i.e.UPS, Courier, or US Mail). The trick is to find the different distributors.

By far the easiest way to locate distributors is to talk to a friend that works for an auto parts store. He would be able to get you the names and phone numbers of a few places very quickly. Since there are many distributors both large and small, there is an advantage in getting the names that the auto parts store uses — they have probably determined which are the best over their years in business.

You can also look in the Yellow Pages under Automotive. They could be under a number of different headings (depending on your phone book) but first look under *Automobile Parts and*

Supplies - Wholesale and Manufacturers. Make sure you search through a few phone books from the nearest cities. Most of the distributors are found in metropolitan areas, not in small towns. They will send you their product line catalogues and pricing sheets upon request.

There is one last way to get big discounts on auto parts. Did you know that eight million cars are processed by the U.S. Salvage Industry every year! This provides you with an opportunity to buy perfectly good used parts at <u>50% or more below retail prices</u>. If you have a good local auto wrecker, he will have a satellite system to locate parts all over the country for you in minutes. It is a great place to pick up just about any part, but the most popular are alternators, pumps, engines, transmissions, rims, body panels, etc. Many auto wreckers offer warranties on their parts.

For example, the engine in a Jetta Turbo Diesel was on its way out. I went to a wrecking yard and bought a 1990 Turbo Diesel engine with 15,000 miles on it for $900; less money than it would have cost me for an engine overhaul, much less an entire new engine. It may be an option you want to consider. Hint: all auto wreckers will wheel and deal heavily if you stand your ground.

THE ENGINE I BOUGHT FOR $900
WAS ORIGINALLY PRICED AT $1500!

In the last two tips for using your business to buy parts at a discount, you are also <u>entitled</u> to the dealer pricing that any supplier offers. You will be surprised how many nationwide suppliers offer dealer pricing. This will allow you to get about 20 - 25% off on specialized parts where you would normally have paid the full retail price.

In summary, you can get 20% off all your parts if you "cut a deal" with the auto parts store owners. You could also start buying many of your parts from an auto wrecker at 50% or more savings. Or, of course, you could also open a business out of your home and qualify for up to 40% off all new parts. I personally recommend opening your own business because it is so easy to do.

It is simply a matter of filling out a few forms at city hall and paying a small registration fee. The tax benefits alone are worth the entire process, but why not make a few dollars on the side? This is how I got started at age 17. I was going to sell a few parts to my friends to pay for my own sporty modifications that I wanted to do. To make a long story short, things skyrocketed, and I turned a small business from the basement of my house into one which did a quarter of a million dollars in sales (per year) within two years of start up. You can too! I am sure you have more intelligence, experience and know how than I did when I was 17 years old!

Just think how easy it is to rack up a few sales. Think how many cars there are per family — usually two and sometimes three. Let's say that two of your friends need a set of tires for their car...

YOU SAVE THEM 10%-15% OFF RETAIL PRICE AND YOU CAN POCKET AROUND $150

Not bad for a phone call and a trip to your local tire depot. This $150 is very conservative, I used to buy tires at a 50% discount (very common for tire distributor price) and resell them at 20% off. I made $300 for every $1,000 of tires I sold.

I even made a deal with the local repair shop where he would give me 13% commission for any cars I brought to the shop for repair work.

I JUST RECOMMENDED HIM TO MY FRIENDS AND MADE HUNDREDS AND HUNDREDS OF DOLLARS

Your friend goes in for a $500 brake job and you get $72 just for pointing him in the right direction. See how easy it is?!

GET 30% BETTER GAS MILEAGE IN MINUTES
(and ways to reduce pollution to our environment)

It is much easier to increase your fuel mileage than you think. There are many things that affect your mileage in a small way, but when you put them together, they can save you $300 - $700 a year in gas. That could buy you a nice little vacation, couldn't it? I will give you a lot of suggestions; you can pick the ones that suit you the best.

The first thing is speed. Most people do not know that the smallest difference in traveling speed has a very large effect on fuel economy. Traveling at 65 mph (104 kph) instead of 55 mph (88 kph) can waste 17% more fuel. That alone can add a few hundred dollars to your annual fuel bill.

Here are some points:

- Minimize daily warm ups to 30 seconds. Even at sub-zero temperatures, 30 seconds is all a car needs if you don't race away, and make sure to drive the car slowly for the first few miles. The rest of the time you're wasting gas.

- Higher octane gas (super unleaded) does not give your car more power or better fuel mileage. It means your car is more resistant to detonation. Purchasing the more expensive, higher octane, premium fuel provides no benefit to most cars. The only reason to use high octane gas is if your car is starting to "ping" (which is also called engine knock). This knock will not only rob your car of power and fuel mileage, but more importantly, depending on the severity, can ruin your engine over time.

- On the highway, use cruise control to reduce gas consumption. It helps maintain a steady speed and therefore better gas mileage.

- Don't fill the gas tank to the brim. Stop when the pump clicks off. Usually, tanks have overfill tubes and when you go around a corner with an overfilled tank, some gas spills out through this tube.

- Check tires regularly. Under-inflated tires can run hot and shorten the life of the tire and rob you of mileage — up to 4% for every 5 pounds it is under-inflated. Air expands with heat, so when inflating a warm tire add about 4-5 psi to your recommended tire pressure. In addition, for every 10% your tire is deflated, you increase tire wear 15%.

- Some people over inflate their tires to get less rolling resistance and therefore better fuel economy. It does work, but there is a catch. You can get premature and uneven tire wear and end up replacing your tires much sooner than normal. The money you save on gas is more or less the same as the added expense of replacing your tires much sooner.

- Use your air conditioner sparingly because your engine has to power the air conditioner compressor. By using the air conditioner, you can increase your fuel consumption by 10% on the highway, and up to 20% in stop and go traffic.

- Some companies are marketing a product termed a "gasbooster" that retails between $25-$100. Each product uses the principle of ionizing the gas with a new gas line material or using the heat from the water hoses to help vaporize the fuel/air mixture. The product manufacturers claim a 3-5% better fuel economy and can reduce pollution by up to 15%. I have personally tested many of them, and **they did not live up to their promises**. There may be one out there that works, but I haven't seen it yet. And if these products are so great, improve fuel consumption and reduce pollution, why isn't every car manufacturer putting them on their vehicles?! It would only cost them a dollar or so in mass quantities.

- Many major gas companies or retail and department chain stores offer a percentage discount from your gas bill if you purchase gas on their credit card. Usually they will give you between 5 cents to 15 cents per gallon (depending on the total quantity purchased over a month). **This can really add up at the end of the month.** Just inquire the next time you are filling up at your favorite service station.

- Save up to 1.5% by removing unnecessary items from the car (commonly in the trunk). For every 100 pounds in extra weight, the car eats up 0.5% more gas.

- If you have a carbureted engine, a poorly tuned car can use 5-9% more gas then normal.

- Save up to 4% by taking your snow tires off as soon as it is safe to do so.

- You can save up to 5% by removing roof racks that create wind drag.

- Use premium multi-grade oils to save up to 5% on your fuel consumption. Friction modified oils can improve your mileage. Use low viscosity oil in the winter, like SAE 5W30 or 10W30. Also, start using EC (Energy Conserving) or EC II grade oils. EC oil reduces fuel consumption by up to 1.5 - 2.7%.

- Try to conserve the car's momentum. It takes 600% more gas to move a car from a dead stop compared to one that has a couple mph's momentum. By observing traffic conditions and maintaining a reasonable distance from the car ahead of you. This will reduce braking and allow you to keep the car's momentum. The gas it takes to accelerate from 0-35 mph in half a city block could have carried you a half a mile at 35 mph. Simply getting out of poor driving habits can save 10-25% in fuel expenditures.

- Radial tires can cut 3-4% of your fuel bill.

- If you own a pick-up truck, remove your tailgate (or put it down) for any highway driving. The tailgate acts like a drag chute giving you very poor fuel economy as much as a 15% loss). If you don't want to remove your tailgate; you can use a soft net-type gate or get a bed cover to almost eliminate the drag chute affect.

- Expect up to 10% drop in fuel economy in heavy rains, and 1-2% for every 10 degree Fahrenheit drop in temperature.

- Fuel consumption is heavy in the first 20 minutes after start-up, especially in winter months, because the car hasn't fully warmed up to its efficient temperature. To reduce this effect, use a block heater. Purchase one with a timer so it comes on

2-3 hours before you have to start the car. A warmer engine means easier starting and better fuel economy. This also reduces pollution to our environment since the car's emissions are much higher before it warms up.

- Avoid driving with an open sunroof or windows at highway speeds. It increases aerodynamic drag and wastes fuel (up to 8%). Use the vehicle's flow-through ventilation to provide fresh air for passengers.

- If you are going to be stopped for more than 60 seconds with the engine idling, shut it off. It takes more fuel to idle over 60 seconds than it does to start the car.

- Make sure your front wheels are aligned properly. A misaligned front end increases fuel consumption.

- Keep filters and catalytic converters clean. Dirty filters increase fuel consumption as much as 10% and studies have shown that **33% of all vehicles** on the road are in need of a new air filter.

- A V-8 engine averages 17.5% greater fuel consumption than a V-6 (that could amount to as much as $500 per year in fuel savings). A four-speed automatic gives you 5% better fuel economy than a three-speed automatic transmission. Consider this when buying a car.

- Also, when buying a car, it is good to find out if it has a lock-up device in the torque converter. If it doesn't, it means there is probably always slippage, which can increase fuel consumption by 6%. The lock up reduces this slippage and saves wasted energy.

- An automatic transmission will have an average of 5-11% poorer fuel economy than to a 5 speed manual transmission that is used properly.

- Most people don't know that power steering can add 3% to fuel consumption with its added weight and strain on the engine.

- By driving in a straight line instead of letting the car wander from side to side in the driving lane, you can save up to 2 mpg.

- **A new car that is "broken in" properly can get as much as 5% better fuel economy throughout its life.** Refer to the owner's manual for "break-in" procedures.

- When you go to foreign countries, many do not have gas pumps that reset to zero after each use. Many unsuspecting tourists are fleeced when they pay for their own gas and the gas registered on the pump before them. This is very common in Mexico. Don't end up paying for 50 liters of gas instead of the 30 liters you actually pumped.

- If you do an excessive amount of traveling, you may consider changing your final drive gear. You might want to get a low axle ratio gear so that the car's engine can turn the wheels faster at the same r.p.m.; therefore getting better fuel mileage. This lower final drive ratio is sometimes an option when buying a new car.

- Cars are usually "air-starved" at high speed. If you do a lot of highway driving it may be worth your while to use a homemade air ram. Purchase a length of air duct, similar to the type under the dash of your car, and attach one open end behind the front grill so air is forced into the tube. Cut an opening in the air cleaner intake and attach the other end of the air duct with sheet metal screws there (you can use duct tape to seal the connection if you wish). This will achieve better fuel mileage at highway driving speeds if your engine is "air-starved".

- **A fantastic tip used by truckers everywhere is to purchase gas on Indian reserves**. You can buy gas at 25 - 40% discount because there are no taxes on gas on the reserves. Most maps mark Indian reserves clearly, and many times they are just a few miles from major interstates. Plan your trip to stop and fill up on reserves and save big dollars.

- Split Fire® plugs claim to give you 4.8% better gas mileage and a smoother running engine. Although you will probably see a slight increase in gas mileage, it is not guaranteed. I don't think it will be as high as 4.8%. We didn't notice any significant difference in our test car, but feel free to try it; maybe you will find a difference.

- Converting to propane is another alternative. Although this is an expensive project, you will save approximately 30 - 50% on your present fuel cost (depending on local propane fuel prices). With this type of saving, the conversion process could easily pay for itself within a year. After that, you are saving 30 - 50% for doing absolutely nothing but using an alternative fuel. Because propane is considered a cleaner fuel, it can mean smoother acceleration and idling, reduced engine maintenance, overall improved performance and less air pollution (carbon dioxide, is partially responsible for the greenhouse effect). As you may already know, most taxi cabs are converting to propane or natural gas. Tokyo has been using this system to improve air quality for many years now.

- Consider buying a diesel engine next time you are in the market for a new car. The disadvantages are: the initial purchase price is more, it's noisier and has less horsepower. The advantages are: much greater fuel economy (usually 25 - 30%), higher resale value and maintenance is lower due to a more simple engine. The best customer for a diesel engine is one who drives more than 15,000 miles a year. If lack of power is a concern, try a turbo diesel. They have about the same horsepower as a gas engine of the same size.

Expect to get poorer mileage on short trips, in cold weather, or heavy traffic — this is normal.

Studies have shown that you can save 15% on gas just by practicing simple maintenance and driving habits. If you use all the other tips and techniques, you're looking at much more savings.

Remember, that the less fuel we burn the better; for the sake of the environment. With over 200 million cars on the road just in North America alone, the pollution effect is astronomical.

In Case of Emergency — It is late at night, it's 50 miles to the next open gas station, and you have only one gallon of gasoline. If your car gets 20 mpg, you know you won't even come close to making it. Well, you *can* drive that 50 miles on one gallon of gasoline. Here's how:

This is a simple technique used by Mileage Marathon drivers. Accelerate very slowly to 20 mph, turn off the engine and shift the car into neutral. Let the car slow to 5-8 mph, restart the engine and repeat the process over and over again. Make sure your flashers are on as not to cause an accident and keep alert for someone coming up fast behind you. This technique is incredibly effective but should be used only n an emergency situation.

HOW TO BEAT POLICE RADAR AND LASER TRAPS

I do not condone breaking the law. But I do believe that some new speed enforcement measures have been introduced by the government solely as a "money grab"; not to increase safety and reduce accidents as they claim. This is especially true with photo radar. You have a right to protect yourself from illegitimate enforcement techniques.

There are many different types of radar. They operate on different frequencies and have different trigger mechanisms. You have probably heard terms like 'K',' X', and 'Ka band', 'instant-on', 'laser', or 'photo radar'. All of these will be explained.

Without getting into technical terms, a radar works by sending out a signal from the "gun" which reflects off your car (or more precisely, the metal of your car) back to the radar gun. The "gun" measures this signal to determine how fast you were going. They are very accurate if used properly.

There are 5 bands that it operates on. They are the X, K, Ka, Superwide Ka and Laser bands. If you purchase a radar detector and it is missing any of these, you are leaving yourself wide open (however, currently laser is rare). Radar detectors aren't the best way of protecting yourself from radar guns anymore. What a detector basically does is pick up the radar waves the police are transmitting and warn you that there is a radar gun nearby. Radar detectors can pick up a very weak signal; sometimes two to three times further away than the police radar gun can detect you.

However, lately the police have begun using instant-on guns much more. These are guns that are warmed up, and all the operator has to do is point it, pull the trigger and he gets a speed reading before you know it. Since the gun isn't actually transmitting any waves until he pulls the trigger, your radar detector will not pick it up until it is too late. The only defense against this is to hope your detector will pick up the short burst of waves that the police officer aimed at a car in the vicinity. Nevertheless...

THE OFFICERS KNOW THIS AND ONLY USE THE GUN IF THEY VISUALLY JUDGE THAT SOMEONE IS SPEEDING.

Instant-on radars are only found in stationary police vehicles on the side of the road or in ambushes. But this type of speed enforcement is disliked by many officers because it is time consuming. The officer has to park, roll-down their window and "zap" motorists. Most cruiser-mounted radars are constantly on when the police vehicles are in motion or when stationary. If they are stationary, they can just turn on the gun and do paperwork, etc. until the alarm goes off telling the officer that a speeding vehicle is approaching. But, since they are constantly on, it makes it easy for radar detectors to detect them.

People don't usually contest the accuracy of the radar gun, most just plead guilty and pay their fines. Many are not even convinced of their own guilt, but do it anyway. For all you know the gun may not be accurate or the officer may have "clocked" another vehicle thinking it was yours (this is quite common!). But before we get into contesting a ticket, let me show you how to avoid one.

Police can only "clock" you if you are coming directly at them or directly away from them. For every degree angle you are away from them, your speed displayed on the radar gun will decrease, because it can only read motion directly towards or away from the gun, not sideways. This is a very important point. That is why you look for police directly in front of you on the side of the road, on an overpass, etc. Refer to diagram A and B.

A real controversy, lately, is photo radar. It seems to be stirring up a lot of debates. It is used in selected areas throughout North America. Basically, it is a radar gun mounted in a mini-van that detects your speed and takes a photograph of your vehicle. You

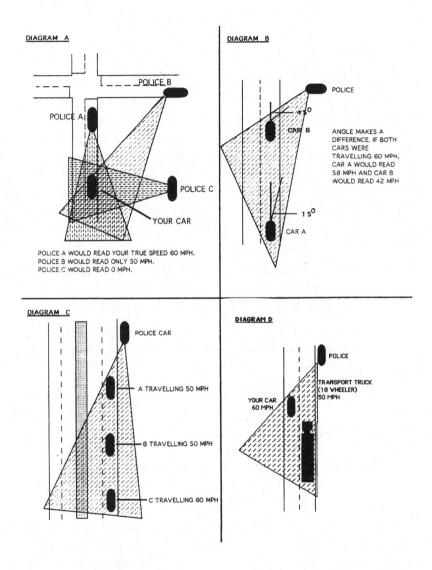

DIAGRAM A

POLICE B

POLICE A

POLICE C

YOUR CAR

POLICE A WOULD READ YOUR TRUE SPEED 60 MPH.
POLICE B WOULD READ ONLY 50 MPH.
POLICE C WOULD READ 0 MPH.

DIAGRAM B

POLICE

45°

CAR B

ANGLE MAKES A
DIFFERENCE. IF BOTH
CARS WERE
TRAVELLING 60 MPH,
CAR A WOULD READ
58 MPH AND CAR B
WOULD READ 42 MPH

15°

CAR A

DIAGRAM C

POLICE CAR

A TRAVELLING 50 MPH

B TRAVELLING 50 MPH

C TRAVELLING 60 MPH

DIAGRAM D

POLICE

TRANSPORT TRUCK
(18 WHEELER)
50 MPH

YOUR CAR
60 MPH

are then mailed a speeding ticket with the photo of your car and license plate. Currently, depending on your state, most of them:

1) operate on the Ka or K band at a 22-26 degree angle
2) "clock" you from the front or rear of the van then snap a picture when you pass in front
3) <u>do not</u> report your conviction to the DMV or your insurance company.
4) can operate when in motion or when stationary

Since photo radar only emits 0.5 to 2.0 milliwatts of microwave energy (compared to 20 to 100 milliwatts from a normal police radar), your radar detector will only pick it up at about 450 feet (the unit snaps a picture at 100 ft). This is a very short distance at highway speeds. To give you an example how effective photo radar is; in a police force of 29 officers, there were 4050 speeding tickets issued for the entire year, (approximately 11 tickets every 24 hours).

PHOTO RADAR UNITS IN THE SAME AREA
ISSUED 700 SPEEDING TICKETS
WITHIN A SINGLE 24 HOUR PERIOD!

This is a blatant "money grab" justified by the government under the guise of road safety while **they are taking in millions of dollars in revenue**.

There is a way to defeat them. If the photo radar unit clocks you from the rear of the van, it calculates (by your speed) where you will be when you pass so it can snap the picture. If you slow down dramatically as soon as you notice the unit, the unit will be taking a picture of where it thinks you will be when you pass the van; but since you have adjusted your speed, the picture will be of a blank road as you will be "behind" the picture area.

If the unit clocks you from the front, you can (if you are attentive), spot the vans on the side of the road and have time to check your speed before passing in front. Remember; you must keep very alert.

"Laser" is another big conversation topic in speed enforcement. There are very few units in service now (about 3,000), but they are tough to beat. It is used in almost every state on a limited basis.

The laser gun is almost like a real gun, in that you have to aim it directly at the car you want to "clock". It uses a narrow, tightly-focused laser beam instead of microwaves like the X, K, and Ka band radar. Unlike radar, which can't distinguish one car from others in close proximity, a laser operator can pick out your car in heavy traffic. Also, unlike radar which fans out and reflects off trees, buildings, signs, and over hills, the laser beam, (which only gets 6 feet wide at 1,000 ft.) is almost impossible to pick up with a detector until you are "clocked". In other words, if your laser detector goes off (excluding false alarms), you have just been hit by a cop aiming at your car.

However, it has been found that powerful lights can sometimes diminish the laser beam's effectiveness long enough for your detector to go off and allow you to check your speed. Weather, such as fog/humidity/cloudiness can reduce the effectiveness of the laser (as low as 100 feet). Also, contoured cars as well as dark cars (such as black, brown, blue) do not reflect the beam as well as more square and lighter colored cars. These characteristics do not apply to radar.

The advantage on our side is that laser is a very time consuming speed enforcement method. The laser beam has to be separately aimed at each car like the instant-on radar guns. But unlike radar, the beam is so thin you literally have to track the moving car for a few seconds to get a reading, making it very difficult.

OK, let's get back to regular X, K and Ka radar bands.

If you are using a radar detector, don't put it on your dash with a baseball cap or kleenex box over it. Cops look for this.

There are myths that putting tin foil in your hub caps or dragging chains from the back of your car will make it harder for the radar to pick up your speed. **These are completely false!**

However, there are a few things that can disguise your car from radar. One is a stealth bra. It looks like a normal car bra but has materials that absorb radar waves, not allowing them to "bounce" back to the police radar gun as easily. Assuming you are being "clocked" from the front...

YOUR CAR IS INVISIBLE TO THE RADAR GUN UNTIL YOU ARE VERY CLOSE TO IT.

By that time you have noticed the police car and have checked your speed.

Another disguise is the actual car you drive. The radar gun is fooled by fiberglass or composite bodies like Corvettes or kit cars. This material masks the metal so it is harder to pick up your car until you are <u>very</u> close.

Radar needs large quantities of metal to bounce off back to the radar gun with a strong signal. You can use this to your advantage by "masking" your car with others. (diagram C). In this situation, the police officer cannot clock you because the radar will pick up car A which is closer and bounces back a stronger signal. You will not be clocked if you stay behind car B or weave in and out of traffic, moving your way up, but staying behind the car in front of you for as long as possible, for "cover". However, once car B passes the police car, you are in full view of the radar. Hopefully by then, you have noticed the police car and have checked your speed.

In diagram D, the speed of the transport truck will show up on the police radar gun, <u>not</u> you. Even though you are closer to the radar gun, because he has a much larger surface area of metal, the signal returning to the radar gun is much stronger than yours.

In other words...

BY PLANNING STRATEGICALLY WHERE YOU ARE ON THE HIGHWAY AND STAYING WITHIN CLOSE PROXIMITY OF OTHER CARS, YOU CAN USE OTHER CARS TO BLOCK YOU FROM BEING "CLOCKED".

Another way of avoiding radar traps is to use what I call a "runner". If you are in a hurry and someone goes zipping past you, let him get 1/8 of a mile ahead and move up to his speed. He will be caught in any speed traps ahead. Although this is not a foolproof system (sometimes there will be two officers waiting for both him and you), it generally works great.

Most police officers will ignore speeds slightly over the posted limit. Many have threshold speeds. These are speeds in which you may be over the speed limit, but they will not stop you. For example in many states, although the speed limit is 55 mph on a four lane highway, you are not likely to get stopped unless you are above 65 mph. But beware; that threshold speed may drop to 60 mph on a tighter two lane highway.

Be on the lookout for police on crests of hills, around corners, on the top of overpasses (near an exit ramp), behind overpasses, obstructions, parked cars and on the side of the road with their trunk open (the trunk lip is used to hide their patrol lights). Learn to recognize these traps and check your speed accordingly.

HOW TO TALK YOUR WAY OUT
OF A TRAFFIC TICKET

Most of the information I am about to reveal to you has been recommended by retired police officers. So take it seriously! Some of what follows may sound silly, but it works!

COMMUNICATION IS THE KEY.

The better you understand the police officer's point of view, the easier it is to avoid a ticket.

The only sure way to beat a traffic ticket is to obey all the signs and laws. However, the police understand that it is difficult to obey all traffic laws at all times.

If you are going to talk your way out of a ticket, it is going to depend mostly on your *attitude*. You want to be friendly and polite without seeming like you are trying to "butter him/her up". Your attitude should be one of "I'm not so sure what I have done wrong, but the officer surely had a good reason for stopping me". You should be at his mercy, but also wanting to discuss the situation.

Keep in mind that you do not know what frame of mind the officer is in or what events have taken place lately. For all you know he/she is in the best mood because he/she just got voted police officer of the year. Or, he could have just found out his wife is cheating on him. The reason I am mentioning this is because it is so important that you maintain a good attitude. If the officer approaches you with an overbearing attitude and you decide to tell him what you think of it, you can bet you'll get the ticket.

By the way...

THERE ARE NO SUCH THINGS AS QUOTAS.

However, there is an expectation from the supervising officer that the officer writes the same <u>average</u> number of tickets as any other officer would on the same shift, location, and with similar traffic conditions.

So here are some of the Do's:

1. Pull over as soon as possible. You don't want to annoy him.
2. Politely inquire as to why you were stopped. However, if your violation was so obvious a child could have seen it, ***don't ask.*** You might say "I'm sorry officer, I didn't see that traffic sign until it was too late".
3. Never admit to the speed you were "clocked" at.
4. Never admit that you didn't know how fast you were going.
5. Ask the officer if he clocked your speed on the radar. And politely ask if you could see the reading.
6. Always sign the ticket, it is not an admission of your guilt, just a promise to appear in court.

Things you should never do when being stopped for a traffic ticket:

1. Never say, "You can't give me a ticket, I haven't done any-thing wrong"! The officer will take this as a challenge and you will <u>surely</u> get a ticket.
2. Never say, "I have had four tickets — if you write me one more I'll lose my license"! This shows the officer that you are a bad driver and should be taken off the road to make it safer for others.
3. Don't argue over the violation. It is OK to tell your side of the story, but ***do not*** get the officer on the defensive. He will only justify to you (and himself) why you deserve the ticket.
4. Don't tell the officer you'll take it to court. There are two reasons for this: first, he will take it as a challenge and further incentive to write you the ticket; second, he will prepare himself by taking detailed notes regarding your vio-lation so he can beat you in court.

5. Don't cry. It works on occasion for women, but never for men. Most cops feel that people who cry are trying to gain their sympathy and will refuse to let this affect them.
6. Don't use "I know the (important person)"! Although this occasionally works, you are taking a <u>big</u> risk. Most cops take it as a challenge or a sign that you think you are better than him or above the law. Or maybe (for all you know) he hates the person you just mentioned.
7. For women, a raised skirt or an unbuttoned blouse doesn't always work.

Excuses that don't work:

1. "Officer, I am almost out of gas, I was speeding so I could make it to the next gas station"!
2. "Officer, I dropped my sunglasses on the floor and when I picked them up I must have gone through the stop sign".
3. "Officer, I had to hurry, my little girl has to go to the bathroom"!
4. "Officer, I don't understand it, my brakes weren't working properly and I went through the stop sign. Don't worry, they seem to be OK now".
5. "Officer, I wasn't speeding intentionally. Once in a while, my gas pedal sticks". Never blame your car for your violation.
6. "Officer, I didn't know there was a bottle of rum in the car, my wife must have left it there"!
7. "Officer, I am glad I found you! A car passed me going extremely fast, I was trying to catch up to the car to get his license plate number. Did you see him"?

These 7 excuses generally do not work. However, you can "work" with an officer if you give him a reasonable and compassionate excuse. Many times they will let you go with a warning.

Seven excuses that work extremely well:

1. "Officer, I have a perfect driving record. If you just give me a warning this time, I will do my best to keep it that way".
2. "Officer, I had no idea what I just did was illegal. If I had known, I would not have done it. Could you let me by with a warning? I will not let it happen again".
3. "Officer, I'm sorry, I should be paying closer attention. My boyfriend/girlfriend just broke up with me and I am having a hard time keeping my concentration on other things. I probably shouldn't be driving right now. I promise, I will be more careful".
4. "Is there something I can say or do that will make you not write a ticket and just give me a warning this time"?
5. "Officer, I know this situation is completely my fault. I should have known better. Can you excuse me this time? I promise you will not have to stop me again"!
6. "Officer, I am normally a very safe driver, I don't know where my attention went for a second. Could you let me off with a warning? I promise I will be more careful in the future".
7. "I'm sorry, I didn't realize I was going that fast until I saw your flashing lights. I guess I was concentrating on where I was going, not what I was doing. Will you excuse me this time? You have just made me realize it has been a long trip and I need to stop for coffee".

If your violation is very serious, it may be better to be cooperative and not say as much. Let the officer do all the talking until you get a lawyer.

There is one other excuse women use that can work well, but it is a blatant lie and I personally don't agree with it, "If I get a ticket, my boyfriend will beat the crap out of me".

Police sometimes have prejudices against sports cars or teenagers. Not because they are mean cops, but they watch them much closer than the average car, since on average they break the traffic laws more often.

In the sports car situation, a cop will watch a sports car more closely because they are designed for speed and handling. That makes it more probable for a speeding violation. Also, these cars are stopped for more minor offenses because they attract more attention to themselves compared to a normal car.

In the case of a teenager, police understand that they are generally energetic, enthusiastic and impulsive and can be prime candidates for speeding or traffic violations. Also, many teenagers have a chip on their shoulder when they get stopped by a cop. This is why so many teenagers get tickets when they are pulled over. Remember, attitude is the key to talking your way out of a traffic ticket.

If you are being pulled over and light up a cigarette, the cop may assume that you have been drinking and are trying to mask the odor on your breath. This is very common. Quickly popping in a breath mint or breath spray will have the same effect.

In most normal traffic violations, when the officer goes back to his car, it is all over. He is going to write the ticket. Once the ticket has begun it is next to impossible to reverse the process.

If you are in a collision, avoid talking about the accident with anyone but the police. Do not make incriminating statements like "it was all my fault". It is the policeman's job to determine who is at fault, not yours. It is very difficult to talk your way out of a ticket when it involves a collision. In most cases the evidence will point to the one at fault.

There is one last battle ground left... the courtroom. Surprisingly enough...

MANY CASES ARE WON BY THE DEFENDANT IF THEY ARE WELL PREPARED.

Since a traffic ticket can affect your wallet and your insurance rates, it may be well worth the time to fight it in court. You can expect the actual proceeding to take only 10 to 15 minutes. However you may have to wait half the day to get your turn.

Many times people get lucky because the officer does not make it to court that day; so the case will be dismissed and you don't pay the fine. It happens <u>quite</u> often. This is also a reason why you <u>don't</u> tell the officer that you plan to contest it in court when you are getting the ticket. He would definitely know to show up on that day.

Preparation for your day with the judge is the key to winning. The idea is that you want to plant the idea in the mind of the judge that the officer has made a mistake or you weren't completely at fault.

We will use a speeding ticket as an example since they are the most common.

It is important to take photographs of the scene — any roadway sign or marking that may be relevant. Make sure to obtain the officer's name, and his partner's (if applicable), and which officer was driving.

Other important details you should write down are:

- at what point you noticed the police car
- what were the driving and lighting conditions (dust, dawn, rainy, foggy, heavy or light traffic)
- what cars were in close proximity to you
- what direction were you traveling in
- were there any roadway or traffic signs, or obstructions

When you step into the courtroom, the officer will tell his side of the story. If you notice any inaccuracies, point them out to the judge later. You will then have an opportunity to ask the officer some questions. The more questions he cannot answer accurately, the more doubt it puts in the judge's mind about the events that really took place that day.

Some examples of questions you may ask the officer in a speeding violation are:

- Where was your patrol car when you first noticed my vehicle?

- How many feet were you from my vehicle? (you could have calculated that it was impossible for him to see you at that distance if you come prepared with notes of hills, road signs, obstructions, etc.)
- Did you notice any other vehicles at that time near me? (if there is a larger vehicle near you, he could have clocked him on radar instead of you)
- What were the weather conditions like?
- How was the traffic?
- Was your radar gun tested for accuracy? If so, when?
- Have you been trained to operate this type of radar gun?

Don't argue! Point out the inaccuracies to the judge later.

You will then tell your side of the story and the officer will have a chance to ask you questions. Answer promptly and accurately. This will impress the judge and strengthen your case.

If the officer's case is no stronger than yours, commonly the judge will rule in your favor because he/she has seen the trouble length you have gone through to present your case.

If you are going to take your violation to court, I recommend you attend a couple of cases in a courtroom to see how the system operates. You will be much more comfortable and have an advantage when your court date arrives.

Here's an interesting fact:

ONLY 5% OF TRAFFIC TICKETS GO TO COURT AND 50% OF THOSE ARE REDUCED OR THROWN OUT!

I personally do not have the time to fight a ticket, so anytime I have received one, I have hired a traffic ticket consultant from the yellow pages. These are usually retired police officers who, represent you in court for a small fee and fight the ticket for you. I like this method because it is not the money that bothers me when I get a ticket, but the points I lose on my license and the effect it has on my insurance rates. I am willing to pay a lot of money in order to keep these points. Busy people might want to consider this option.

There is one last resort if you go to court. In some states, if you lose your case, you can plea-bargain for traffic school. This generally means you will still have to pay the fine, but by attending one day at a traffic school, you avoid having your conviction reported to the DMV, therefore preserving your license status and insurance rates.

SERVICE CENTERS AND HOW THEY REALLY OPERATE

It is my job to show you the mistakes that could be made, the pitfalls, and the "bad apples" of the industry you might meet when repairing your car. It is difficult to reveal all of these disturbing incidents without coming across negatively. It may even sound like I am saying that the entire industry are a bunch of crooks. There are some who *will* take advantage of you, but for the most part, if you don't present an opportunity for them to cheat you, they won't. If you know the pitfalls, you can avoid them. This chapter may scare the hell out of you, so please keep in mind what I just said as you read on.

Some repair centers are famous for ripping you off. They often have a service-with-a-smile motto, being as friendly as possible while grossly overcharging you for the service you receive.

I sometimes think I should have entitled this section, "The Great Automotive Rip-off". Did you know that the Federal Trade Commission estimates that

20 BILLION DOLLARS IN AUTOMOTIVE REPAIRS EACH YEAR ARE <u>UNNECESSARY?!!</u>

This is partially due to fraud and partially the incompetence of the mechanic. The major dilemma now is that almost everything on the car is tied into the "Black Box". You almost have to be a computer engineer to service a car. The on-board computer (sometimes called the "brain box", or ECM) is constantly monitoring your car's performance and adjusting itself to be more efficient. This offers many advantages, such as better engine performance, improved fuel economy, reduced air pollution and the extension of maintenance intervals. However; it makes it **almost impossible** for backyard mechanics to do their own repairs (other than strictly mechanical work like brakes and suspension). Still, even simple repairs like brake-work are changing due to the sophistication of anti-lock brakes, etc.

Since many of us do not understand even a fraction of the terminology used in car repairs anymore, it's a *perfect opportunity* for service centers to take advantage of us. The kicker is...

MOST OF THE TIME YOU WILL NEVER KNOW IT!

Before we go through different service center tactics, your first step is to get a repair shop manual for your car. This is such an important step, because you can **probably avoid about 50% of the rip-offs** or unnecessary work by familiarizing yourself with your car; where the various parts are, and how they operate. It only takes about two hours to skim through a manual. Chilton and Haynes offer very good ones which can be purchased at almost any automotive shop or department store.

You have made a substantial investment in your car, and you pay a lot of money to fix and maintain it. So you want to know more about your car than the fact that it has a key you turn to start it.

By learning what the different parts do, you will understand what the mechanic is talking about, and can determine if he is suggesting a sensible repair. The other reason to read the shop manual is that when you tell the mechanic what the problem is, he will realize you are not a complete novice when it comes to nuts and bolts. In turn, he most likely *won't* take the risk of suggesting you replace unnecessary parts, which is one of the biggest problems in the industry. With this knowledge you can describe the problem better (for more efficient repairs), and will probably have a general idea of what it may be, again **lowering the risk** of being taken advantage of. It makes **much more sense,** to lower the odds of being ripped off and to educate yourself in prevention. It saves money and hassles in the long run.

The most susceptible customer is the one who doesn't understand anything about a car. If the mechanic sees this, he knows that whatever he says the car requires you will probably accept (because he is the expert, right?!). You trust his recommendations, right?

REMEMBER, IT IS THE SERVICE CENTER'S JOB TO SELL YOU *WHATEVER* POSSIBLE BY WHATEVER *MEANS* POSSIBLE!

Don't take that lightly — it's the **truth**. The unfortunate part is that some centers actually step over the line and lie so that you spend more money.

Before I go any further, I want to clear up a major myth. Fram, a manufacturer of oil and air filters, did a survey and determined that approximately one million new car buyers were told that they must have all the repairs performed at the dealership or their warranty would be void. This is <u>wrong</u>!! The truth is that all simple repairs and maintenance items including oil changes, brakes, etc. can be repaired elsewhere without voiding the warranty... so stop paying high dealership prices for these items.

Although there are honest shops with integrity and high standards, they are **few and far between**. Any time you have your car repaired you have a good chance of being ripped off. Later in this chapter I will explain how this happens, who is targeted, and how to find a good, trustworthy mechanic. We will also discuss certain types of shops that are better at certain specific repairs.

Much of that $20 billion in wasted repairs is due to lack of communication between the service center and you. The weakest link is the Repair Order (RO). A typical case would be the following. The service advisor writes on the RO "Transmission shifting wrong". The mechanic looks at the problem and writes this "Checked transmission and road test, no problem"... and you get a $60 bill. This is a concern because you shouldn't have let the service advisor get away with what he wrote. There should be specifics, i.e. "Transmission shifts are too long in higher gears after car is warmed up". This tells the mechanic want to look for.

There is also a second reason for this. If your transmission breaks down after your warranty expires, and you are armed with a few RO's complaining of specific problems, you can get repairs done **free of charge** after your warranty has expired. We will later discuss why this is a **VERY** common occurrence and how the dealership may be setting you up by claiming "no problems found" on the RO. It is absolutely imperative that you get a good description of your problem and specifics on the diagnostics. Don't let "transmission working to specification" or "unit works normally" suffice. This will be explained later in the chapter about getting free repairs after your warranty expires.

Before we discuss the different service centers available and which you should use, let's talk about a good mechanic.

POOR AUTO MECHANICS FAR OUTNUMBER THE TRULY COMPETENT ONES!

Truly competent mechanics are hard to find, but it is worth the effort to locate one - the money and grief you save will be your reward.

Ask friends and co-workers for someone they recommend. It will give you a good place to start.

There are many ways to evaluate a mechanic, but at a bare minimum, he should be Automotive Service Excellence (ASE) certified. They certify in eight categories: Brakes, Engine Repair, Front End, Tune-up and Emission control systems, Electrical systems, Air Conditioning and Heating, Manual Transmission, Rear Axles and Automatic Transmissions.

A good mechanic frequently attends training courses sponsored by different suppliers and manufacturers in the industry. Check to see if these certificates are recent. This is very important. As you know, the technology changes in the last few years have been rapid and countless. It is next to impossible to keep up on the new equipment **unless** you are trained.

A KNOWLEDGEABLE MECHANIC CAN SAVE YOU HUNDREDS OF DOLLARS WITH PROPER AND EFFICIENT DIAGNOSTICS OF YOUR CAR'S PROBLEMS!

"But this is so simple", you say. You will be surprised at how many mechanics do not have any of these certificates; or if they do, how outdated they are. Most of them do not want to give up a day of pay to sit in class. And to complicate the problem, many shop owners don't want to send them because they are not willing to give up the few hundred dollars in labor hours that the mechanic would make for the owner that day. They don't seem to grasp that the payoff in customer satisfaction, getting repairs done more quickly will be beneficial in dollar amounts, that they will have a better mechanic (and service department) and therefore a much happier clientele.

It can even get worse. Some require almost none or no qualifications to work on your car. For example, in Georgia right now, you do not have to be trained at all to work at a repair center. *Your mechanic could have been a butcher a few days before working on your car.*

Of course, the standard way to evaluate a repair shop is to call the Better Business Bureau, the Department of Consumer Affairs, and possibly even the Attorney General's office to see if there are an unusually high number of complaints.

At the service center, look around the shop and the office. Is everything clean and well kept? If the shop is sloppy, you can bet their work is too.

Ask if the shop maintains a library of technical service bulletins. These are bulletins distributed by the car manufacturers and consist of technical updates, special repair instructions and servicing hints on different cars. No mechanic can effectively work without these bulletins. They are not found in any service manual. Without these repair bulletins to assist repairs, a shop could easily charge two to five times more in wasted time, and still not correctly fix your car.

You might also want to check if the service center belongs to the American Automobile Association (AAA — or the CAA in Canada), or the Automotive Service Association (ASA). These organizations set certain standards and guidelines for members, who are considered to be more reputable than non-members.

But no matter what qualifications they have, if you are getting a lot of run-around, techno-babble or double talk, take your car somewhere else.

We will discuss two more very important (but sneaky) methods of evaluating a repair shop in the "Secrets of Buying a New Car" chapter.

OK, time to get into the good stuff.

Can you trust the mechanics you have been doing business with? Many people think that doing business with a particular repair shop for years provides insurance against being cheated. The scary part is that **without a doubt**...

MANY SHOPS ONLY HURT THE CUSTOMERS THEY KNOW BEST!

Why? Because you are so unsuspecting that you become an easy target. Also, since you have done repeated business there, they know you are not an undercover law enforcement officer from the Department of Motor Vehicles posing as a vulnerable customer. The DMV often 'sabotage' their cars and pose as helpless customers in order to accurately judge if a service center is repairing the vehicle fairly.

There are usually two basic methods the repair shop uses to set you up.

The first is when the repair center charges very little for their work the first few times to get you to become loyal and trusting. This practice portrays them as an honest, reliable, and cheap repair shop. Then once you are a repeat customer, they will **either cheat or overcharge you**. [By the way, the words "honest" and "reliable" are almost never associated with a cheap repair shop. If you want good service, you usually have to pay for it, but I will show you ways around that later.]

The second system is where the customer is charged heavily for the repairs done, but treated very courteously in the hope that they will return. If the customer returns, this process is continued a few times. On the third or fourth visit, they will charge very little for an expensive repair. You, the customer, are led to believe that now that you are a 'regular', you get a magical discount. You think "what a nice guy my mechanic is". You are now very loyal to the shop and return often, under the assumption you are now getting a special price for your repeat business. Sorry to say, some will take advantage of this and overcharge you **every time** from now on.

How do mechanics overcharge or cheat? I will discuss specific shams and scams in another chapter, but to give you an overview of some of the trickery that goes on, the next few pages will describe a couple of ways.

The most notorious is that...

YOU ARE CHARGED FOR PARTS THAT NEVER HAVE BEEN REPLACED!

You may have been charged for a set of rebuilt brake calipers when they have merely been washed off with solvent. Or maybe your car is burning oil, so they charge you for an expensive piston ring replacement (or ring job as they call it), **when in fact** there was only a simple valve stem seal replacement done. They will go so far as to wash off some of the parts with solvent to make them look as if they were removed, apply a bead of silicone around the oil pan to make it look freshly installed, or even mark the bolts to make it look as if they have been removed. Don't be concerned, these are not common scams. They are only done by the outright crooks.

So, how can you protect yourself?

First, ask for **all** your old parts back. If the mechanic tells you some of them have to be traded in when buying your new rebuilt parts, he is probably telling the truth. But this only applies to buying rebuilt parts like alternators, brake calipers, etc.

Tell the mechanic that you want to keep track of which parts on your car are Original Equipment of Manufacturer (OEM) and which one's are aftermarket, so you would appreciate it if he could place the old parts in the empty boxes of the new parts being installed. This deters the mechanic from replacing your parts with used or rebuilt parts but charging you the price of a brand new one; without accusing him of being a crook.

In some areas there are strict laws governing auto repairs, but most people (and repair shops) are not aware of them. For example, in Canada, by law, the repair center <u>must</u>

1. Keep all old parts for 90 days
2. Have VIN# of you car on the repair order (including oil changes, etc.)
3. Have a <u>written</u> estimate for all repairs
4. Have estimate signed before repair begins (no phone authorization is legal)

These have fallen by the wayside because they were never enforced, but if you do get ripped off you can use them to show how the repair center broke the law. This will be great assistance in getting your money back! So check the laws in your area at City Hall — you may be surprised.

Another defense is to occasionally police your mechanic. You can so this by placing a small mark or scratch on the parts that may require replacement. You can even take a hammer and small punch to make an indent on the part and cover it over with grease and dirt. Later you can look for the mark to confirm that the part has been replaced.

OK, on to the next stage — billing rip-offs. There are two types of time billing, the Flat Rate system and the Clock Hour system.

The Flat Rate system is probably the **most** abused. A manual listing the average time it takes for a repair is used. You are supposed to be charged the number of hours found in the manual multiplied by the hourly labor rate — *no matter how long it takes the mechanic to do it*. Sounds pretty fair, doesn't it?

The first problem is that there are two manuals to get this average time calculation from; aftermarket manuals and factory manuals. Factory manuals are what every manufacturer gives its dealers to bill the factory for its warranty repairs. Aftermarket manuals are published by independent sources and allow much greater length of time for each repair. In correlation, *you pay more.*

The time allowed in the aftermarket manuals is almost always unrealistically high — but a real profit generator for the service center. They tend to take into account older cars with rusted or seized parts, and a mechanic with average working skills and normal hand tools (no power tools), therefore taking longer.

This is big business. Under the flat rate system, if the job takes the mechanic 1 hour but the flat rate is 1.6 hours, he gets paid for 1.6 hours for doing one hour of work. More importantly, you get charged for 1.6 hours of work.

THAT IS WHY MECHANICS AND SHOP OWNERS LOVE THE FLAT RATE SYSTEM!

They can get paid for a 12 or 13 hour day when they really only worked 8 hours. I personally know many flat-rate mechanics making $45,000 to $70,000/year; even a few as high as $110,000/year. Hard to believe, isn't it?

[This also reminds me of something. When talking to mechanics or service technicians, and you want to reduce your chances of getting ripped off or overcharged, try using the terminology "re and re" (i.e. "How much to re and re that alternator?"). That's short for "remove and replace". They'll think you know what you are talking about and think twice about fleecing you.]

The Clock Hour system is where you are charged for the actual time it took to do the repair. It is the most fair type of billing, but is abused when it comes to diagnosing. Generally, if a mechanic must search for the cause of a problem, they will charge you per hour. Many will claim that they have no idea how long the problem may take to locate; so many consumers allow unscrupulous or incompetent mechanics to take hours and milk them of their money.

This can lead to the "camp out" or "hood up" sham. This is where the mechanic has the hood up like he is doing something to the car (or maybe giving the illusion that a test is running), but in reality *nothing* is really being done — other than adding hours to **your** repair bill.

Although it's true that it is not easy to accurately estimate how long it will take to find a problem, there is always a maximum amount of time that can be allotted to diagnose your car.

Other common rip-offs are the "leave it with me" or "hook it to the scope" scams. With computers and the diagnosis equipment now available...

MOST ENGINE PERFORMANCE PROBLEMS ON NEWER CARS CAN BE DIAGNOSED IN 30 MINUTES TO AN HOUR!

Most mechanics would <u>love</u> to be paid for three hours of labor when only one was done. This is pretty tough to do if you are watching over his shoulder. But if the mechanic gets away with telling you, "the problem will take a while, so leave the car with me", he now has the opportunity to charge for those extra hours. This "leave it with me" line is also used when the mechanic really has no idea what the problem is. He doesn't want to show you his lack of knowledge as he fumbles around the car with repair manuals.

Don't finance the mechanics education; that's what certification tests are for.

If you **must** leave the car, ask for a written estimate and limits for diagnostic time. Keep in mind that some shops may ask you to leave the car because of their mechanics' schedule, or if they are just plain "booked up".

Computer "scopes" or "engine analyzers" are *very* important in the automotive industry. Make sure your service center has one. They cost $40,000, so you will be surprised how many don't have one. Small hand-held analyzers cannot do the tests that a "full" engine scope can. They can quickly diagnose any late-model car, but be aware that they can intimidate an unwary consumer so the shop can overcharge. It takes about 20 minutes for the computer to go through all the tests, including time for the mechanics to interpret the print-out. There are a lot of flashing lights and meters that make it look like this machine is doing an awful lot. Since you figure something important must be going on, the mechanic can leave the car on the scope for a hour when the test really only took 20 minutes. Remember that most engine performance repairs can be diagnosed within one hour, **so don't be swindled into paying for extra time.**

Also, make sure to get a printout of the tests. This verifies that a "full" scope was actually done. Many times the scope will be busy, so the mechanic uses hand-held analyzers but charges for a "full" test. Getting a printout will prevent this.

Another tip is to mark down the mileage on the odometer before you leave so you can verify that a road test has actually been done after the repairs.

Let me give you an example of unnecessary repairs and over-charging that happened to me personally. It is **so important** that you understand some of the nuts and bolts of your car. With a little common sense you can spot these rip-offs a mile away.

Around December 1993, I brought my car into one of the largest automotive repair chains in Canada. They informed me while doing a routine check on the front end that my brakes should be replaced. The mechanic invited me out to the shop to inspect my car. He pointed out that the front brake pads of my Z24 had about 30% wear left on them and should be replaced **immediately.** Well, I first noticed that there was more like 40% pad wear left, but didn't say anything. Next, I asked him how long they would last. He wouldn't give me a time until I repeatedly asked him. He then replied they **may** last until the end of the month, but that I *shouldn't* take the chance.

I did a quick calculation in my head. Most metallic brake pads should last for 30,000 miles at an absolute minimum even when used extremely hard. So let's see, 30% of 30,000 miles is 10,000 miles (and remember there was more like 40% left). . .

What this mechanic was trying to tell me was that I was going to put 10,000 miles on my car this month - I THINK NOT.

With those calculations, which are very generous in the mechanics favor, the brakes should have lasted about nine months since

I put about 13,000 miles on my car each year. I kept quiet and kindly asked them to put the wheels back on take the chance.

In April 1994 I decided to take my car in to get those pads replaced. When the wheels were taken off there was still 20% pad wear available. It's funny that the car that wasn't supposed to make it until the end of December went another five months with **lots** of room to spare. The moral of this story...

NEVER BELIEVE ALL 100% OF WHAT MANY MECHANICS SAY!

Next, I'll take you through the advantages and disadvantages of different service chains and independent repair shops. First let me describe another experience I had at one of the big muffler/brake chain locations in New York State. I brought a Jeep in for extensive brake work (of course these people advertise "free brake inspection").

The idea behind this "free inspection" is guilt. They hope that after putting your car up on a hoist and looking at it for a while, you will feel guilty about putting these people through all the trouble and purchase the recommended repairs. They make it difficult for you to say "no" by being **very** friendly and courteous. Remember it is a lot harder to say "no" to a friend, and they are counting on that. Besides, you are a easy target — why else would you want a brake inspection unless you suspected something was wrong? Again, your frame of mind is in their favor.

To make this story short, the mechanic called me at home after his inspection. He stated that he couldn't believe I even drove the Jeep there in one piece (we will talk about this tactic in a later section). I needed a complete new set of brakes for approximately $980, and new ball joints for another $300.

Well, knowing how they operate, I said I would have to think about it and call them back in a few minutes. They reminded me that my Jeep was tying up a hoist and that they needed it so I should call back right away.

I think they were quite aware that I was going to call around for other prices, and they obviously didn't want me doing this.

I called a garage that I felt I could trust and got a price. **Wow!** It was $740 for the brake work. I called the shop where my Jeep was and claimed I didn't have the money right now for the repairs and that I would have to put the Jeep in storage until I could afford it (an obvious lie on my part). I instructed the mechanic to put the vehicle back together and I would be there to pick it up in a while. He then told me I could get away with not replacing the ball joints for a little bit, but that the brakes have to be done now. He immediately asked me to hold on for a minute. The mechanic returned to the phone claiming he had just talked to his boss, and he was willing to offer me credit terms to pay monthly.

They must have wanted this business <u>bad</u>. Well, of course they do, they are making $200 more in pure profit than the repair shop just down the street.

I told him that I believe in paying cash and never take credit. He turned into and **instant** salesman making me a better offer (willing to come down $50). I declined and picked up the Jeep.

I drove that Jeep (that he couldn't believe made it) into the shop two hours away, to a mechanic I could trust that does honest repairs. He did the <u>same</u> repairs for $731 ($250 cheaper than the big muffler/brake chain store) and claimed my ball joints were in **perfect shape**; so there was no need to replace them (another $300 in savings).

Luckily, I didn't assume that just because this company was a big discount chain that their prices were great and I wouldn't be taken advantage of.

THE ORIGINAL ESTIMATE OF $1250 REALLY ONLY COST ME $731 (A SAVINGS OF $519). NOT BAD FOR A COUPLE OF PHONE CALLS!

Do not be afraid to shop between different repair centers; you will find that some prices can vary drastically. Here's yet another example: I saved an instant $59.85 by making a few phone calls. Instead of my muffler costing me $132 (which I was quoted by the first place I called), I spent $72.15 by taking my business down the street. Not bad for a few minutes work!

That brings up a very important point. **Do not diagnose your own car and ask for a specific repair**. Repair centers <u>love</u> this. Let's say you come in and say, "I need a tune-up". The mechanic will be happy to give you one, but will that fix the problem? Maybe you have a plugged catalytic converter, and a tune-up was <u>not</u> what you needed. You received and paid for one because you asked for it. After you have wasted that money, the mechanic probably would have pointed out that you need a new catalytic converter (after the tune-up). The most important thing is to **communicate with your mechanic**. Let him tell you what is wrong and judge his recommendations from there. Too many people pay for repairs they never needed.

Different repair centers have advantages and disadvantages. There are generally 5 types of businesses offering automotive repair services: department stores, car dealerships, automotive retail chains, service stations, and small specialty shops. Let's go through them each in turn.

<u>DEPARTMENT STORES</u> (ie. K-Mart, Sears, etc.)

Many department stores have learned that some repairs are very profitable and can be fixed while a customer is in the store shopping. Most of these chains specialize in a few major repair items that are profitable, and that do not extend beyond their mechanics' technical experience. Because of their volume buying and aggressive competition, good deals can often be found at these shops.

They also tend to push their own brand name products first because they are generally less expensive and have more profit margin for the store. If you want a specific brand, make sure you ask for it; otherwise you'll be getting their brand name the majority of the time.

Department stores usually have set prices for each job calculated by the clock hour system explained before. However; be aware that most stores offer commissions or a bonus system if a mechanic or service technician sells more parts and service above a certain quota. This **can** lead to dishonest business practices. For example, I was at a smaller department store chain doing research for my book when I saw the service manager dash across the shop to ask what the mechanic was doing. The mechanic replied, "just rebuilding a brake caliper". The manager angrily rebutted, "We don't rebuild calipers, we sell new ones! I want to see a new set on that car right away". As you can see, unless you know that your calipers can be rebuilt, **you will pay** for a more costly new set.

Remember, **these mechanics at the "quick-stop shops" are only trained for the simple repairs they specialize in.** These places are **absolutely** great for those repairs, but if they offer you any services above that, thank them very much and take your car elsewhere for the additional repairs.

THE CAR DEALERSHIP

The dealership has received a bad rap lately; and it is well deserved. However, it is not as bad as people exaggerate it to be.

Let's talk about the good side first. Generally, the tools and equipment are state of the art and their shops are always clean and professional. They have larger parts stock, specialty shops (like paint and body work) in the same building, separate detailing crews, well-coordinated staff and beautiful lobbies where you wait. All of this is great and dandy, but you are paying **dearly** for this "professionalism". This is <u>definitely</u> the most expensive type of repair facility!

They charge much more for "original parts" and their service technicians are usually paid on a flat rate manual system. This system is much more profitable for the mechanic and the dealership. Since the mechanics are much more familiar with your make and model than generic mechanics because they are continually exposed to the same cars, they can spot the problem faster and get the job done in less time. But you still pay the full rate from the flat rate manual. This is where they make big bucks.

The dealer's hourly labor charge can be as much as <u>double</u> that at a local independent repair shop. First, their employees are probably the **most** qualified technicians in their area of specialty. Second, they know they can get away with it because they are considered the "experts" on your car. Finally, they have to pay for the expensive tools, modern surroundings, extra specialty crews, etc.

These technicians are supposed to be the best because of their "factory" training. Usually they are trained this way, but this is not always the case. The problem isn't the training, but the mechanics' attendance at it. A greedy dealership can't stomach losing seven hundred dollars in labor sales on a mechanic who spends a day in school. Besides, most dealerships would rather spend the money for colorful new flags to advertise their used car lot rather than training their mechanics. Some just can't see how it pays off in the long run. That is why you <u>must</u> check how recent their certificates of training are. They may post ones that are 5 years old (it looks great on the wall). Unfortunately, much of the technology has changed since then and that information is almost useless.

The main reason that new car dealerships are looked upon so harshly is not just because of their high prices but the plain fact that when they work on your car under warranty, they are usually confronted with a difficult troubleshooting task. You can get the idea that the dealers are incompetent because they take so long and may have to repair your car multiple times to get the problem finally solved. Keep in mind that you give them the **hardest** tasks like intermittent problems or electrical problems which are very difficult repairs. The independent repair center has it <u>much</u> easier. Their job is usually routine maintenance or "re and re" of parts — again, very easy repairs; no hassles, no complaints. But because there are less headaches with the independent shop, you have the **illusion** that they are better.

If you give the same easy repairs to a dealership, with their state-of-the-art equipment and better-trained mechanics, they will usually do a better, higher quality repair. But, of course, you will pay much more for that repair in comparison to an independent shop.

I recommend that regular repairs like oil changes, muffler work, smog checks, regular maintenance checks, radiator work, tires, alignments, and brakes not be done at the dealership. They just cost too much.

AUTOMOTIVE RETAIL CHAINS (ie. Midas Muffler®, Goodyear®, Penzoil Pit Shop®, etc.)

These are the places that claim usually they can perform a simple service while you wait.

The rates often charged at these quick stop shops are very competitive due to aggressive competition. They are generally based on a "package deal" when it comes to services like brake work, muffler work, tires, tune-ups and oil changes. They advertise these package deals which look very attractive. But beware, anything that falls outside of the package (or extra) will be charged for **very heavily.**

Before you become too upset with this practice, remind yourself about how almost every airline advertises a $99 super saver fare for a flight, but **only** a few seats are available at that price. Or how about the lawyer whose "hassle-free $200 divorce special" **almost always** turns into a $7,000 - $10,000 expense over a year.

For example, if you are getting an oil change and they check your car to find you need a new air filter, you will pay dearly for that filter. That is how they make their money. How else, when they only charge $15-20 for an oil change?

Retail Chains should only be used for what they are respected for and specialize in (i.e. muffler work for a muffler shop, brake work for a brake shop, tires and alignments for a tire shop). This is because of the technical level of the mechanics employed here — we are talking entry level. Once the mechanic becomes extensively trained and certified, he is likely to move on to a better paying shop.

I say this because, lately, some chains have been offering services that their mechanics are not specifically trained for in order to take up market share.

The advantage to these chains is that they can offer highly discounted prices because of the volume they do in a specialized area. However, keep in mind that they can keep the prices low because they deal almost exclusively in replacement parts and commonly use rebuilt or reconditioned parts. Make sure you are aware whether new parts have not been installed on your vehicle or not.

The automotive chain is usually an independently-owned and operated franchise, and **not** regulated or monitored regularly like the big department store chains. Also, it usually has a quota system which it must meet every month. This can lead to over-charging or unnecessary repairs — so be aware.

With this aside, these outlets are **very good** for the repairs they specialize in.

SERVICE STATIONS (ie. Mom & Pop type gas stations with a few repair bays)

This is where the auto repair industry really started. In recent years, most existing stations have closed down because of the invasion of high volume chain stores. There are still a few of them left, but the majority are only good for very minor repairs since their technical knowledge is limited as are their tools and equipment.

There are a few exceptions to this rule. Stations that are really a independent specialty shop with a few gas pumps outside for extra income are fine.

The type I recommend you stay away from is the independent gas station that has tried to open a repair shop in the adjacent bay. These people are to be used only for emergency work and very small repairs like fan belts, hoses, batteries, minor tune-ups and oil changes.

You want a can of STP brake oil or radiator coolant? They will be happy to sell it to you at 50 - 100% higher than the auto parts or chain stores. Remember, they are not discount volume shops.

One very comforting fact about being small is that the customer satisfaction rate is much higher than in almost every other type of repair facility.

SMALL SPECIALTY SHOPS (ie. Independent shops sometimes specializing in certain cars)

These repair facilities offer a "go-between" for quality repairs without the high dealership prices. They have the proper, and sometimes specialized, tools and equipment to do repairs efficiently. They are usually owned independently by an ex-mechanic or ex-service technician/manager. They usually offer general repairs to most makes and models at reasonable prices. Most will have less than four mechanics on staff, and some will even have state-of-the-art equipment (like $40,000 computer scopes), just like many of the big franchises.

If you own a foreign or exotic car, these shops can be a **life saver**. Although technicians at any given repair center may be trained on foreign automobiles because of the demand, you are stuck many times with bringing the car to the dealership for quality repairs. That is where these specialty shops come into play. They are also frequently exposed to the same cars (or same component), so chances are that they can make speedy repairs, usually with less error.

One hint is to talk to owners of similar cars and ask where they get them repaired. For example, in my city there is a little-known independent specialty shop that specializes in repairs for Porsche, Audi, Jaguar, and Volkswagen for a fraction of the cost at the dealership. They advertise in a small community paper so they are not well recognized; but just ask any Porsche owner and they will know about the shop for their car.

You will find that their prices will always be below dealership costs by a substantial amount; but never as low as the retail chains or department stores. But then again, most of the chain stores will not stock parts for your foreign car, or for that matter, competently repair it.

After discussing all of the different repair centers and their advantages and disadvantages, the real question becomes **"where do the best mechanics work"?**

Don't let a few bad experiences with warranty work be your only basis for judging the dealership. You may feel that the better mechanics are at independent shops, but the opposite is often true.

Dealerships pay higher wages and give more benefits which are attractive to good mechanics. They also have state-of-the-art equipment, and being associated with the factory makes it easier to obtain technical information. But as you know, you have to pay more for work from the dealership.

There are exceptions to this rule. Sometimes very good mechanics or managers with the entrepreneurial spirit from dealerships or automotive retail chains will open their own shop and provide excellent service. This is where the independent shop has a <u>definite</u> advantage and can be your **best bet**. The owner of an independent shop usually takes a personal interest in his mechanics because he knows the costs of recruiting, training and keeping the interest of a good one. This provides for low employee turnover and...

LOW EMPLOYEE TURNOVER IS PROBABLY THE BEST INDICATOR AS TO WHERE THE BEST WORK IS DONE!

You will also tend to get the most courteous treatment and personal attention at a smaller independent shop. Also, because the credit card companies charge the merchants (<u>not</u> the cardholders) 3-5% when the customer uses his credit card, many shops will give you a 3-5% discount if you pay in cash. **Just ask for it!**

One of the most successful ways to protect yourself at a new repair center is to ask to see the service manager aside for a moment. Explain to him that you are new in the area and looking for a good mechanic to take your "best interests at heart". Who would he recommend? This implies that you are aware of some overcharging in the industry, and are willing to trust him and keep your business there as long as he keeps treating you honestly and fairly. It also makes the mechanic's ego go through the roof when you ask for him specifically. It may sound trivial, but it means a lot to them. You will find yourself getting little freebies all the time — like free lubes, wiper installation, etc.

With this aside, *don't let low prices be your first concern*. Some people are really attracted to the "low-ball" advertising on car repairs they see. These ads often mention quality work done inexpensively. This is rarely true. If you want quality repairs with quality parts, you usually have to pay for it.

One common practice of "low ball" pricing is to use inferior replacement parts to bring the total repair bill down. Remember, **the inferior part will have to be replaced much more frequently and actually cost you more over the long run**. Don't think I am saying that all aftermarket parts are junk. In fact, the majority of them are better than the factory original equipment. The name Fram (manufacturer of filters) is a perfect example. Just make sure you are aware of the brand name that is going into your car.

What about the big chains and quick stop shops? Are they any good? Definitely! Just remember to only get work done in their area of specialty — anything out of their advertised packages will be **very expensive**. Examples of these chains are: Midas® or Meineke® for mufflers, Goodyear® or Firestone® for tires and alignments; AAMCO® or Mr. Transmission® for automotive transmission work; Mr. Lube® or Penzoil Pitstop® for oil changes...the list goes on. Automotive specialization is the wave of the future; if the chain becomes known for a certain specialty, do more volume, and can then offer bigger discounts. It's tough to beat many such prices.

As a side note, I want to warn you about something called switching. It is a practice found in a few small independent repair shops. This is where you have been quoted and billed $46 for each new set of Wagner® brake pads (4 sets per car) but they actually used Red Stallion® or no-name pads which are worth anywhere between $6-20.

THEY JUST MADE A CLEAR PROFIT OF ABOUT $120 FOR DOING ABSOLUTELY NOTHING EXTRA (OTHER THAN BEING DISHONEST)!

As mentioned before, the way to beat this is to ask the service technician to keep all the old parts in the empty boxes of the new parts being installed; or ask him to write down the brand name of the installed parts on the invoice or repair order. Some shops are now doing this automatically.

The bigger the city, the more you will find outright rip-off shops! If you break down away from home (especially in a big city), beware that "small time" tow truck operators get cash kickbacks from the work done to your car from the repair shop they recommend and take you to. Of course, they will take you to the repair shop where they get paid the most; probably a rip-off shop that will charge you more. You are easily victimized by someone who seems to be offering friendly advice on where you should take your car for repairs.

To be safe, always call a CAA, AAA, or your auto club tow truck. Ask to have your car taken to a <u>credited</u> major car dealer. You may pay a little more than at an independent shop, but you will most likely get fair repairs.

Again, I apologize for the tone of this chapter seeming so negative. Although most repair centers are not crooked, there are many who will sell you everything they can whether the repairs are necessary or not. There are a limited amount of honest, good repair centers. They are the people who will try to fix something instead of replacing it, are concerned about spending your money on expensive parts and try to find an alternative, and only repair what is needed. These places are hard to find and always in demand.

I don't mean to scare you with this chapter. Just beware of what *can* happen. It is a tough business world out there right now. *Primetime* (the TV news journal) did a story on one of the large auto repair chains. The local franchise owner blatantly admitted that he was recommending and replacing a lot of small parts that weren't necessary. His justification was that sales were down $10,000 already this year (it was only February), people were being tighter with their money, and most of all, he was getting a lot of pressure from head office to keep sales up.

One last pointer: if you have a problem like sticking lifters, a small radiator leak, a slight oil seal leak, etc., make sure to try one of the "quick fixes" at the local autoparts store. What I am talking about are the bottles of additives that you can buy that claim to stop leaks, or stop sticking valves, etc. These products will not always work, but <u>sometimes</u> they can solve your problems. It is worth the $4-$6 purchase price, and **may save you an expensive repair.**

WHO WILL GET RIPPED OFF?

There tend to be certain types of people who are more likely to get ripped-off, so we will go over some of them.

The "Family Man" is a prime candidate. He is the type of person concerned about family safety and does everything 'by the book'. He is most likely to follow the recommendation of the manufacturer or dealership. Service technicians use common lines like ..."well, the manufacturer recommends it" or maybe "look, the life of your children are riding on those brakes, it's safer to get them changed now". This provides an opportunity to lead the customer into unnecessary repairs.

Single professionals are other prime candidates. They really set themselves up by stating that they are in a hurry and just want the problem fixed. Sometimes they might even say, "no matter what it costs, just fix it now". Successful professionals (commonly executives) often have many things on the go. His or her lifestyle, business and social commitments always take priority and the repair shop can use this to their advantage. One way to avoid this is to dress down when going to the service center and play down your self-status or importance.

Women have also always been taken advantage of in the repair industry, although this has been curbed lately due to women informing and educating themselves about cars. The way a woman dresses will be a major factor in determining how large her bill will be in an unscrupulous repair shop. If she walks in with high heels and a business dress claiming "something funny happens when I press on the pedal", you can expect that bill will be adjusted accordingly. A women should never flash her credit cards, should never show her lack of automotive knowledge, or that she is hugely inconvenienced by the car's breakdown and wants it fixed immediately. She should also dress down and play down her self-status or importance as well.

IF YOU COMBINE ONE OF THESE "TYPES" OF PEOPLE DESCRIBED ABOVE WITH OUT-OF-STATE PLATES, YOU ARE ASKING FOR TROUBLE!

When a dishonest mechanic notices your out of state plates he knows that he will never see you again and <u>now</u> is the time to "scalp" you.

If you are one of the three types of people I just mentioned, there is a little trick to intimidate the mechanic so they don't dare take advantage of you. Bring a repair manual with you (found at any auto parts store) and make sure the service manager sees it in your hands. You can place it nonchalantly on the service desk when you fill out the repair order. It is also a good idea to flip through the book while you are sitting in the waiting room. You may not have any idea what you are looking at, but the service manager or mechanic doesn't have to know that!

You would probably think that Senior Citizens are the most likely to get ripped off. Surprisingly enough, they are often not as vulnerable. Most senior citizens will stay for years with the same repair center as long as they feel they are getting treated fairly and honestly. Also, many of them are on fixed incomes and are more likely to question everything before they sign a repair order. The service manager can't afford to pull the wool over their eyes because he could lose a very loyal customer who will spend thousands of dollars at his shop over the next few years.

Teenagers are also not that susceptible to dishonest practices. First, they are usually hard to fool because many of them are automotive enthusiasts. Secondly, most of them don't have enough money to fill the gas tank, much less pay for light car repairs. And lastly, they will openly argue the smallest repair bill if they feel they have been rooked in any respect. Unfortunately, many service managers have a tendency to refuse the work because of the potential headaches, especially with teenagers who have brought in their modified 'hunks of junk.' Common excuses are, "The car is beyond our specs. Our policy won't cover that", or "none of my mechanics will touch that".

By the way, if you are a teenager and your parents are paying for the repairs, make sure your <u>don't</u> let the repair shop know. Their entire story will change, and you may get taken.

OIL CHANGES FOR LONGER ENGINE LIFE
The Truth About Miracle Oil Additives

Beware of low-priced oil change bargains. You will notice that the price will <u>drastically</u> go up with the addition of useless additives and extra services not included in the package. Simple things like a $5 hidden oil disposal charge, or an extra $3 for the 23 point chassis lubrication, etc.

Also, most shops have a tendency to include the chassis lubrication that they advertised but forget to check all fluid levels. Make sure to remind the shop manager or mechanic to do this.

As a few side notes on making your car last longer, most manufacturers recommend the engine oil be changed approximately every 5,000 - 7,000 miles (7,000 - 10,000 kilometers).

CHANGING THE OIL SOONER AT EVERY 3,000 MILES (5,000 KILOMETERS) OR EVERY THREE MONTHS HAS A DIRECT EFFECT ON YOUR ENGINE'S LIFE!

Even the AAA agrees with this. Also, ask any taxi cab driver — they put hundreds of thousands of miles on their cars and swear by this.

Now this is more important than ever. Today's engines are much smaller, work much harder and have less oil capacity.

Synthetic oil is also a very good idea for engine longevity. It is **much more** expensive but doesn't break down like regular mineral oils; therefore, it offers **much better** protection and you don't have to change it as often (usually half as often as regular oil changes). Users of synthetic oil have reported as much as 50,000 miles between oil changes (not recommended) and there was little evidence of wear on engines that have logged 250,000 miles.

Synthetic oil has been used in the aircraft industry for over 20 years — they were the <u>only</u> oils that could take the heat and high r.p.m. of the jet engines without breaking down. I have raced professionally for years, and have seen how synthetic oils have taken me through a race where mineral-based oils would have broken down under severe loads and caused engine or clutch failures. This is not to say that mineral oils are not good for everyday use; **they are great**. It is simply that synthetic oils are so much better. Your engine will be better protected against wear, especially if you are hard on it (performance driving, towing a trailer, etc.) For example, any new Corvette or Porsche comes right from the factory with Mobil 1 synthetic oil.

People are becoming more aware and synthetic oils are getting popular. Today, most places stock them. I personally use Mobil 1 or Castrol Syntec; but any fully synthetic oil is acceptable as long as it is the class and weight for your engine (stated in your owner's manual).

Whether you choose to use synthetic oil or not is your choice, but whatever you do...

DON'T USE LOW QUALITY OIL!

Next to your home, your car is probably the second biggest purchase you will make in your life. Some cheap oils still state "meets or exceeds all new car standards". Sure it meets all new car standards when you pour it in, but for how long? These oils do not have the additives the higher quality brands do, and break down very quickly. That is why your oil gets black only a short while after your oil change. You have a lot of money tied up in your car, so don't put "crap" in it.

Also, only use pre-oiled air filters for your car. This reduces the dirt that gets into your engine and destroys cylinder walls (and eventually your engine).

Make sure you determine the brand, weight and quality of the oil you are using. **Not all oils are alike**. Some can increase fuel economy, some stand up longer, and some are designed for hotter or colder weather conditions.

Do not let anyone overfill your engine with oil. It is common practice for mechanics wanting to sell you another quart to do this. Extensive damage to your engine can result. The crankshaft can strike the oil and whip it into a foam (air bubbles), depriving parts of adequate lubrication.

As a side note, used oil from a single oil change dumped on the ground can ruin one million gallons of fresh water — a year supply for 50 people! Americans that change their own oil throw away 180 million gallons of oil every year. **This would provide 113 million gallons of renewable oil if it was recycled!**

What about miracle oil additives advertised on T.V.?

Most of these products have a solid lubricant called PTFE (short for polytetrafluoroethylene) in them. Consumers know this better as Teflon; Dupont's brand name for it. PTFE particles evidently adhere to the metal inside the engine and provide a super-slippery coating to prevent wear. There is some controversy as to whether PTFE particles can adhere to metal with the extremely high temperatures most engines are running or not.

PTFE provides better "slipperiness", but lower friction and superior anti-wear properties of a motor oil can be different. Let me illustrate in an everyday sense. Just because one vitamin pill a day is good for you, it doesn't mean that five vitamin pills per day is five times better.

There are so many different engine and oil treatments advertised nowadays. Many of them do not live up to their claims. There are a couple of good ones out there like Slick 50 and Duralube, but most companies make their products look amazing through a bunch of circus tricks. Many do not even have evidence from an independent lab proving their treatment makes the engine last longer (or whatever it is suppose to do). But the people that make and sell these products sure do their best to imply that. (I might point out that Dupont does not endorse the use of Teflon in motor oils.)

Here are some of the tricks:

One of these company's implied proofs is that as a result these additives, your car gets better fuel mileage. That circus trick is as easy as changing your regular engine oil to a EC or EC II rating (EC stands for Energy Conserving) and you too will get up to 2.7% better fuel economy <u>without</u> any miracle additives.

Another implied proof is how the computer in the car has to adjust to the new "engine environment". This is absolutely true. But what they **don't tell you** is that adjustment may be due to the contamination of the car's oxygen sensor from the new additive. That's right, what was presented to your as a wonderful benefit actually may be doing harm to your emissions control system and...

MAY EVEN VOID YOUR EMISSIONS WARRANTY!

But you may say, "Corey, what about those infomercials showing this miracle lubricant allowing an engine to run an amazing 30 minutes without any oil"? It does not require a miracle to make an engine run 30 minutes without oil. Actually, if the engine is prepared properly before starting and is run in a 'no-load' situation, it is easy. This is even easier if the engine has been fitted with oil-impregnated bearings. Again, **no miracle here**.

Just keep one thing in mind. Some of these treatments are $20-$40, and usually have to be added every oil change. If you are changing your oil every three months, that is $100-$160 per year added to your car expense. Is this expense worth the benefits you are getting from the product?

There are so many products out there that it is difficult to class them all as ineffective without trying them all. It is a jungle out there. There are so many gimmicks to make the test look misleading that it is very, very difficult to tell the good from the bad.

I recommend you stay with a proven product like Slick 50 or Duralube. Although they can make the product sound like an absolute miracle, it is not. However, they do live up to almost all of their claims and you will be generally happy with the results if you decide to use them. They have been tested and proven by independent labs and some of the big oil companies.

One question that probably comes to your mind is: "If there is an oil additive that gives you longer engine life, better fuel economy, reduces emissions, and make your car run smoother; why wouldn't every major oil company start producing a similar product and sell it worldwide? Also, why wouldn't the car manufacturers start adding this additive to the oil in every new car to increase its engine life? They could offer a longer warranty at very little cost to them".

The scary answer is: If the oil companies introduced a product that would allow you to increase your intervals between oil changes and make your car last longer,...

OIL SALES WORLDWIDE WOULD PROBABLY DROP 15% — A COMPLETE DEVASTATION TO THE INDUSTRY!

By introducing a better oil product, the companies would actually be cutting their own throats. As far as the car manufacturers are concerned, why would they want your car to last longer? They need your car to break down so they can supply parts and service — that's where they make their money!

Let me give you a perfect example. Gas tanks were known as an item that probably wouldn't have had to be replaced in the **entire life** of a car. They were a very reliable part.

A few years back, manufacturers started producing gas tanks on new cars with the connecting seams facing inward instead of outward like they used to do (where the two halves of the tank join together). Since the seam was turned inward, there was now a crevasse for dirt, water and salt to collect and help rust-out the tank. These newly designed tanks then sometimes had to be replaced every few years. This caused a *rise* in gas tank sales in the millions and millions of dollars. These tanks are still designed the same today and gas tank sales continue to rise. Manufacturers love the increase in sales — a great good sham if you ask me.

COMMON SHAMS WITH COMMON REPAIRS

I can tell you about all the automotive scams in the world, but the best way to avoid them is to have some idea of what kind of service your car really needs, and how that service can be done in the most economical way.

Beware of scare tactics used by the mechanics when replacing critical parts. They are extremely common and can be <u>very</u> effective in the mechanic's favor. What I mean by scare tactics like "your life is riding in this car, it is not worth the risk, just replace the part" or "I can't believe your car made it to our shop, you are a very lucky man. Those front end parts are ready to fall apart. You could have had a serious accident". These lines are synonymous with brake work, front end repairs, and tire wear. This is why it is so important to have first hand knowledge about your car. You will be able to tell if the mechanic is being realistic or over-exaggerating. If in doubt, get a second opinion from a mechanic down the street.

How about that "Lifetime Warranty" on the muffler? Wow, this sounds to good too be true, right? Well, it is! They offer a lifetime warranty for as long as you own your car. Do you plan to keep your car for the next 50,000 miles (the approximate life of a muffler)? Remember, you cannot transfer this warranty to the next owner. Even if you do keep it, a few years later you may come in to get a new free muffler under your "Lifetime Warranty"...

ONLY TO FIND OUT THAT IT IS COSTING YOU MORE THAN THE FIRST TIME YOU GOT IT REPLACED!

Yes, the muffler is free, but your are paying premium prices for the pipes, labor, gaskets, and hanger brackets. Also, I am sure they will find another part of the exhaust system that needs replacing (for a few hundred dollars, of course).

Another great trick is "The Rattle". The mechanic brings you to your car that is up on the hoist, and bangs on the muffler. The muffler rattles as though there are small pebbles resting in the bottom. He says "did you hear that, your muffler is cooked, hear all of metal pieces broken in there! You'd better replace it." All mufflers are exposed to interior moisture and unburnt fuel which causes the interior baffles to rust and corrode. Very small portions break off and lay on the bottom to cause that rattle. In other words, it is *perfectly normal* for the "rattle" to be there.

"The Plug", as I call it, is another sly scheme from the mechanic. This is where he plugs the end of the tailpipe with a rag while the engine is running. He shows you the hissing sound from one or a few of the clamp connections. Don't let them lead you around or tell you it is dangerous because the carbon monoxide could leak into the interior of the car and you wouldn't know it until you passed out. This is a bunch of hogwash! **Any** exhaust system will leak if plugged in this manner. They are designed for flow, not for the kind of back pressure you get when plugging the tailpipe. And even if it did leak under normal use, exhaust gas will not get inside unless you have holes in your floor. The pipes are not passing through the cabin area — they are external.

MUFFLER REPAIR CENTERS LOVE TO SELL YOU EXTRAS YOU DON'T NEED!

The biggest and most expensive part of your exhaust system is the exhaust pipe that starts at the muffler and extends to the back of the car. Many shops claim that since your car has a one piece exhaust system, you cannot replace only the muffler, you have to buy the entire "one piece" assembly from the muffler back. The truth is most repair centers can cut the muffler out with a torch and replace it with a new one by using adapter pipes they normally have in stock.

There is another variation of this scam. I will use my own experience as an example. After being told by my mechanic that I needed a new muffler to pass the safety check, I proceeded to go to a large, reputable muffler chain and get it replaced because my regular mechanic was too busy to do it on short notice. I was quoted a fantastic price of $80 and told them to proceed with the repair. After getting it on the lift, they came back to tell me I needed a new hanger and tailpipe ($150) because they are "paper thin". They invited me out to see the car. The mechanic pointed out that when he cuts out the muffler with the torch he will damage the pipe because it is so thin. I looked at the pipe and it seemed fine (other than the excessive rust that is normal on exhaust pipes). I told him I owned a small repair shop for a short while, and that we replaced mufflers with tailpipes in much worst shape with no problems. I also stated that the car was sold and this muffler was just for a safety check. He replied "Sold? Well, we will try to salvage the tailpipe".

He knew then I had no long term interest in the car and he wouldn't be able to talk me into putting more money into it than necessary. He also then knew that I had it looked at by another mechanic for the safety check and that mechanic did not recommend the tailpipe be replaced. After all was said and done, the muffler was replaced and the so-called "thin" tailpipe was fine. Do you see how easily I could have been swindled out of an extra $150? This would have tripled my bill — a pretty scary expense when the original repair quote was a mere $80.

Brakes can be a great profit generator as well for unscrupulous repair shops. Generally, people know that when your brakes begin to squeal it's a warning sign that they are almost finished and to get them replaced as soon as possible. If you come into a dishonest shop and claim your brakes are worn out (instead of saying there is an odd squeal from them) the mechanic knows you came in prepared to buy a new set of brakes, and **you can bet** whether your car needs them or not, you *will* be getting a new set of brakes.

This squeal is sometimes not caused by worn brake pads, but because the brake got very hot at one point and the pads became glazed, causing a high pitch squeal every time you use them. All that is required to stop this annoying sound is to wash the pads down with solvent and lightly scrub a piece of fine sand-paper across the brake pads and discs (or drums).

This also reminds me to warn you that most Chrysler and imported vehicles <u>do not</u> have this warning mechanism on their braking systems, so they will not squeal when they are worn. Make sure you check the pads at 30,000 miles and every 15,000 miles thereafter. Also, rear drum units usually don't have this type of warning device either.

BRAKE WORK IS ONE AREA WHERE
FEW BARGAINS ARE FOUND!

If you see a really discounted rate, **be skeptical**. If brake work is inexpensive, it is usually due to one of two reasons. First, they could be using inferior parts and cutting corners on labor. Or second, they sometimes promise an inexpensive brake job only to sell you extras that are not included in "the package". These extras are things like machining your discs when it is not necessary, etc.

Ball joints can be used to rake in 'mucho fungolas' from unsuspecting customers since some shops use scare tactics to sell. Some people who complain of front end vibration are talked into new $300 ball joint replacement when a $20 wheel balance would have sufficed. Remember you might have to replace a set of ball joints once in the entire lifetime of your car; not the two or three times they may suggest.

One of my favorite shams of all time is the 'Transmission sham.' Some mechanics are <u>delighted</u> to check the transmission fluid condition or level; **it gives them the perfect set-up for a big dollar sham**. When he takes off the oil pan he shakes his head and runs over to you to show you all the metal particles and sludge in it. "You're lucky you came here now and we found this. It could have cost you a new transmission. All of these metal particles means the internal parts are grinding and shaving off metal. You need a transmission overhaul. It will only be $350, a lot less than an entire new transmission".

Transmissions are <u>supposed to leave</u> small metal particles on the bottom of the pan, it is perfectly natural. Larger particles and shavings should concern you). If they show you the small metal particles and tell you the transmission must be fixed, thank them very much, ask them to change the oil and filter and state you will "chance it" for a while. (By the way, **never** go back there; I guess you assumed that.)

Another great one is when you bring your car in complaining of an absent passing gear or shift timing problem. Devious transmission shops will bill you for a complete transmission overhaul when possibly **only** an adjustment of the shift linkage was necessary.

Consumers are often told that blue smoke and high oil consumption are due to bad valves. Many shops will charge a complete valve job when **only** the replacement of the valve stem seals are needed.

Another "take" on this sham is where you are charged for a rebuilt cylinder head when only one valve is necessary. The only exception to this is if your car has more than 75,000 miles on it and has a burned valve. It is probably a better idea to rebuild the entire cylinder head rather than just fix the valve in this case.

If you ever have any doubts about a shop that you are doing business with, put a small dab of paint or nail polish on the bolts that fasten the parts they will have to take off. The paint must touch both the bolt head and the part itself. After the repair has been done, check if the paint has been disturbed. If not, **get your money back and go to another shop**.

In regard to electrical failures, a voltage regulator is, in many cases, all that is necessary to be fixed. But customers sometimes charged for an entire alternator replacement. Make sure you ask if a voltage regulator will suffice.

Sometimes you can be talked into replacing a clutch because it is slipping, when only an adjustment is needed. Remember, if you come in to a shop expecting to pay for a clutch when really only an adjustment is needed, **don't expect any shady mechanic to try and talk you out of it**. A $500 clutch job is much more profitable than a $25 adjustment. So if it is slipping, have the free play adjusted before you pay for a new clutch.

Cooling systems are supposed to be flushed every now and then to keep the internal build-up down for more efficient coolant flow. Make sure you ask for the entire system to be drained (including the radiator and engine block) and **back-flushed**. If he doesn't do the back flush, you might as well have done it in your garage with a do-it-yourself kit. It is an easy job unless you use a high-pressure back-flush system. So, if they charge you for a radiator flush, make sure they just don't change the fluid and send you on your way.

Have you ever seen the low advertised air conditioning service? It looks great, right?! You get there and ...surprise... they have noticed that you need to add refrigerant (which is overpriced) to charge the system back up. So much for your inexpensive air conditioning service. Most consumers do not question the mechanic's decision to add refrigerant because the mechanic shows you how the air bubbles form in the glass "check" window; and after the freon has been added, they disappear. In actuality, some bubbles or foaming is normal for a car at low r.p.m. (especially idling), so don't fall for that.

Have you noticed that your air conditioning doesn't seem as cold just after you have serviced it?

THAT IS BECAUSE THE SYSTEM WORKS AT 90% OF IT'S CAPACITY WHEN IT IS 50% UNDERCHARGED AND WORKS AT 50% OF ITS CAPACITY WHEN IT IS 10% OVERCHARGED!

Don't let them overcharge the system just to sell you more expensive refrigerant. Make it clear that you want it refilled only to 95%, not any more!

Don't ever be afraid to get a second opinion on any alleged "necessary repair". **I highly recommend it.**

Let me tell you another story that happened to me. I had just bought a used Cavalier Z24, and something extremely bizarre happened. Just after I bought it, the car was running very rough and every time you stepped on the gas hard the car would jerk back (because of the acceleration) and there would be a thump from the front left hand side of the engine. After inspecting under the hood, I noticed that it was becoming spider cracked right above the left front shock absorber.

Could these to two separate problems be related? It looked that way.

I took the car to a large retail automotive chain and asked the mechanic to look at it. Of course he asked if I had ever had service work done there before. I was foolish enough to tell him I was from Ottawa (4 hours away). After taking my car for a test drive he made the following recommendations. The timing belt was probably slipping to make it run rough, and I needed a new front shock. He approximated the repairs at $700. Wow, I thought I just got a great deal on this car, and within one day I have $700 in repairs. Well, I was a little suspicious of this mechanic because what he said did not 'compute'. Besides, the car was just certified (safety checked) a few days before I bought it. So I took my car to another shop.

I said nothing about what they other mechanic suggested or even that I took it to another mechanic. The second mechanic looked at the car for about 30 minutes **and put a huge dent in my ego**. Evidently, the entire problem was a deteriorating set of plug wires. Just by spraying WD-40 on them the car ran better instantly. As far as the spider crack in the hood from the shock absorber; it wasn't even related. It may have been from a deadly pothole the previous owner hit. The thumping sound was actually the car internally back-firing into the air intake which is part of the hood. Because the car's internal back-fire made a popping sound when I stepped hard on the gas, it was muffled to sound like a thump by the design of the air intake system.

The entire cost of repair was a whopping $68.

THIS JUST SAVED ME $632 IN UNNECESSARY REPAIRS!

Wow, <u>did I feel dumb</u>! Here I am, the supposed car expert, almost getting taken for $632 because I let my emotions cloud my reason. I was so upset at being in a foreign city and discovering a major problem just after buying what I thought was a good car I did not think the problem through carefully. It goes to show you, **it can happen to anyone.**

With any repair, always consider getting a second opinion. As with the story I just related, I could have wasted $632. If this happens just a few times, that is a lot of money put directly back in your pocket over the next few years. It is quite common for one shop to recommend a $500 repair when another one would suggest a $250 repair would fix the same problem.

TIRE AND ALIGNMENT
SHAMS AND SCAMS

Many people are sold an expensive wheel alignment when something else is really at fault.

AN ALIGNMENT IS NOT MANDATORY WHEN YOU
PURCHASE NEW TIRES; IT IS JUST A SAFEGUARD

If your old tires were wearing normally, an alignment would be of questionable benefit. So, don't let the service manager talk you into it unless you want it. It can be an easy way to save $100 instantly.

Alignments are also commonly recommended (along with a tire balance) to cure a vibration problem in the front-end. The tire balancing may be your problem, **but the wheel alignment is a total waste of money.** Wheel alignments will correct bad tire wear or steering pull, not vibration.

If your car pulls to one side, but the tires appear to be wearing evenly, the problem may be an internal tire problem. To test this, install the right tire on the left side, and the left tire on the right side. If the pulling problem disappears or appears in the opposite direction, you have a tire problem. Remember to only do this temporarily, as changing the rotation of radial tires is not good for them.

New shock absorbers or ball joints are sometimes sold by deceitful mechanics as wheel vibration cures. The only thing a strut or shock replacement will do is remove the repeated bouncing effect out of your suspension when you hit a bump. **Only in very rare circumstances will shocks or struts fix your vibration problem.** These usually last for 70,000 miles. If they aren't leaking (showing fluid stains), you should be suspicious of a recommendation to replace them. If you have vibration at highway speeds...

ALWAYS TRY AN INEXPENSIVE TIRE BALANCE BEFORE SPENDING A LOT OF MONEY ON POTENTIALLY UNNECESSARY REPAIRS

If you are lured to a repair shop by low advertised alignments and they try to sell you shock absorbers or ball joints, *seriously* think about getting a second opinion.

Other rare causes of the common steering vibrations could be steering linkage problems, out-of-round tires, and non-balanced hubs. However, it could be as simple as having a build-up of mud on the inside of the rims or stuck in the treads of the tires.

I recommend getting your car wheels balanced on a machine that balances them on, as opposed to off, the vehicle. Wheel vibration still may occur after your wheels are balanced off the car because the brake disc or hub may be out-of-balance. A machine that balances the wheels on the car eliminates this problem because the wheel, brake disc and hub are balanced together. **These machines are rare and expensive to use, but worth the extra money when you have a car with a vibration problem.** Keep in mind that since each tire is balances together with the hub assembly, you will not be able to rotate you rims/tires without re-balancing them.

Any time you do an alignment, it should be a four wheel alignment. **Two wheel alignments are generally a waste of money.** You can get the front two wheels lined up, but they may not be tracking properly in relation to the rear tires and may cause excessive tire wear.

RADIAL TIRES DO NOT NEED TO BE ROTATED UNLESS THEY ARE WEARING UNEVENLY, SO SAVE YOUR MONEY ON THIS UNNECESSARY MAINTENANCE ITEM

However, if you do have a front-wheel drive car with a very little rear weight (ie. mini-vans), it is important to rotate your tires front to rear. Failure to do so can sometimes result in a "feather" pattern wearing on the rear wheels, and will ultimately ruin your tires. A symptom may be a sound like a bad wheel bearing — it comes from that feather pattern on your tires.

If you are an aggressive driver, you may want to consider going to lower-profile tires with a wide stance to get more rubber on the road. Someone that is traveling with 70 series tires can move down to a 60 series tire without noticeable difference in ride comfort; but will get better handling characteristics. A general rule of thumb is that all original tire sizes can be increased one size and series brought down one size without changing the rim or having any steering problems. However, your speedometer reading may be affected by up to 10% depending on the size of tires used (ask your mechanic for details on this).

When traveling in winter months, you can lose 25% of your tire life if you don't monitor the pressure. As the weather gets colder, air condenses, therefore giving you less pressure in your tires. A tire that is fully inflated on a warm summer day can drop 8-10 lbs on a freezing day. For every 10 degree (F) drop in temperature, you can expect the tire pressure to drop 0.5 to 1 lb. That's also why you check your air pressure when tires are warm.

Never drive on a flat tire unless your vehicle poses an immediate safety problem. Driving even a short distance at low speed can damage the crucial inner tire surface and ruin the rim.

Spring and fall are the best time for good discounts on tires.

As far as tire prices go...

NEVER PAY RETAIL PRICE FOR A TIRE

They have huge profit mark-up — many times over 100%. Almost every tire retailer will discount.

Unknown to consumers, **many tire warranties include a free rotation in the purchase.** Read your warranty carefully; this item is conveniently forgotten by mechanics quite often.

Also, check the warranty to see if puncture damage is included. Many times the warranty will cover the repair or replace the tire if it becomes punctured. This is another free repair that mechanics often conveniently "forget" about.

It is common to get <u>free</u> wheel alignments. They are an expendable service for a tire shop. If the tire shop salesman thinks he is going to lose the sale of four brand new tires and you will go somewhere else, it is not uncommon for them to offer a free wheel alignment to get your business (depending on the profit margin of the brand of tires you have chosen). Keeping this in mind, when purchasing a new set of tires "hum" and "ha" a bit and then state "I have enough for the tires, but I don't have the money for the alignment and balance. Throw that in and I can afford it". You will be surprised how well this works. They can write off the balance and alignment easily because it is all labor charge. Try it next time you need new tires. Even as a worst case scenario, you will probably get the alignment and tire balance at half price.

Another way to get <u>free</u> wheel alignments is through the growing number of specials around. For example, in a recent promotion, Firestone promised to keep your car's steering aligned, free of charge, through 50,000 miles of new tire use.

1 **Never use reconstituted antifreeze**. It is found on the shelf of almost every autoparts store in America. You are putting your engine at risk by using sub-standard fluid. Stick to a popular brand of ethylene-glycol based coolant. To back up this claim, General Motors published an advisory stating that they are not aware of any chemical that can be added to 'used' coolant to restore it to an acceptable rate. However, at this time, a few companies are working on solving this problem.

2 **If you are buying a used car** and want to find out if it has been recalled by the manufacturer for certain defects or repairs, just take the VIN (Vehicle Identification Number) to the local dealership. They can access the information via computer for you free of charge.

3 **Never run the starter on your car for more that 20 seconds at a time**. It causes extreme amperage draw and can sometimes damage battery cables (even melt the protective insulation down). But more importantly, it can ruin the starter. The starter is only designed for running short intervals and then cool down. So take a one minute break between every 20 second interval of using the starter.

4 **If your engine has ever overheated, the transmission has likely overheated too.** Make sure to change the transmission fluid promptly. It is important to your transmission's longevity. Once the transmission fluid overheats, it loses much of its protective properties.

5 **Tires do not need to be rotated unless they are wearing unevenly**. Unnecessary tire rotation is a common waste of money.

6 **If you feel a pulsation or vibration during braking**, many mechanics will automatically machine your front brake discs. Sometimes this vibration can be your rear drums. To tell the difference, try to notice if the vibration is coming through the steering wheel or through your seat. The steering wheel indicates front brakes, your seat indicates rear drums. You can use this method to also determine the front or rear location of other general vibrations.

7 Keep in mind the **oil pressure light on the dashboard is not a foolproof system**. If the light does come on, the engine has been without oil long enough to do severe damage.

8 If water does not bead up on the car's exterior after it has rained, **it is time for a wax job**. Your car should be waxed twice a year; more if you drive near salt water or park your car outside.

9 **Never get lost on an interstate again**. There is a system to the numbering. One or two digit even-numbered highways indicate major East to West routes. One or two digit odd-numbered highways are major North to South routes. Three digit even-numbered highways are loop routes around a city. Three digit odd-numbered highway head to or from the center of a city.

10 If white smoke flows from your exhaust after the engine warms up, **it could indicate a leaky head gasket** (this is commonly referred to as a blown head gasket). The coolant leaks into the combustion chamber and burns to make the white smoke. Other symptoms to look for are oil in the radiator fluid, or water in the engine oil. Also be aware that white smoke can also just mean that the car is running rich. However, a rich running engine will usually emit white smoke immediately after start-up and continue thereafter.

11 When adding oil to the engine, make sure to wipe away oil that spills on ignition wires. **Oil destroys the insulation on wires, making them weak.**

12 Symptoms of piston ring wear are: hard starting in cold weather, blue smoke from the exhaust, and power loss going up inclines or when accelerating. If you are experiencing these symptoms, be prepared for a "ring job" (expensive). However, worn valve stem seals could also show the same symptoms. If there is constant blue smoke it is probably the rings. If the blue smoke is only during deceleration, it is most likely a seal. **This is a common rip off. They will charge you for an expensive ring job when you only need a valve stem seal replacement.**

13 **If you are trying to locate old service or owners manuals**, contact Dragich Auto Literature 1-800-238-8484 or (612) 786-3925. Also pick up a copy of the *Hemming Motor News*. This is considered the "bible" for any classic car enthusiast. If you're having a problem finding rare parts, this is the book to find them in. It has everything (each issue is usually over 800 pages).

14 **Will platinum spark plugs give you more power?** Absolutely not! The only thing you get from platinum tipped plugs is longer plug life. That's it! So don't believe the hype.

15 Some mechanics will recommend SAE 10W40 for your car when the owner's manual calls for a viscosity of SAE 5W30. In the 1980's SAE 10W30 was the most popular oil. Nowadays, **newer engines have been designed for SAE 5W30**. The only time you should consider SAE 10W30 or 40 is if the temperature is going to run above 90 degrees Fahrenheit for several days or longer. This would then become the oil of choice.

16 Just because a battery says "maintenance free" doesn't mean you cannot add water to the battery like in the old days; most of the time you still can! They usually have a hidden filler neck to add water. **Many times consumers are talked into purchasing a new battery when filling up the old "maintenance free" battery would have done fine** (and saved you $75- $100). However, there are a few battery makes (mostly American made) that are permanently sealed. One of those is the Delco Freedom Battery. It cannot be refilled once it is depleted, it is time to replace it. **Note:** never try to test or charge a Delco Freedom battery that has a clear to pale indicator. This can cause it to explode and seriously injure you.

17 **Most people ruin their door locks without knowing.** Never use lock de-icer without relubricating the lock. De-icer contains alcohol that melts the ice, but it also dilutes the lubricant in the lock thereby causing them to stick and eventually fail. Do not use regular penetrating oil it washes out the lubricant in the lock. Make sure to use a graphite lubricant like *Lock-Ease* or sewing machine oil.

18 **How do I get the musty odor out of my car?** A deodorizer will mask the problem temporarily, and steam cleaning will get rid of it for a while; but it will come back. The trick is to get the carpets and upholstery steam cleaned and then remove the carpets and underpadding to wash the floorpan (the musty smell usually comes from the moisture between the floorpan and the carpet). Don't forget to wash the floor, seats, carpet, headliner and all upholstery with a disinfectant.

19 **Never rest your hand on the gear shift knob;** it causes increased wear and premature failure to the synchronizers. The synchronizers are what stop the gears from grinding every time you shift.

20 **A safety tip: make sure to clean your headlights.** Road salts and grime in winter tend to coat the lights when following other cars and reduce visibility. This may sound unnecessary but try it, it makes a big difference. This is also common in the spring and fall months with wet dirt roads.

21 **Many rear brake repairs could be easily avoided.** A major reason rear brakes wear prematurely is because they aren't adjusted regularly. The great part, which most people don't know, is that by engaging your emergency brake, you move the self-adjusting mechanism in the rear brakes. In other words, by periodically using your emergency brake, you keep your rear brakes adjusted and money in your pocket.

22 **Difficult wiring shorts are the best handled by the dealership**. Most regular repair shops are not properly equipped for this type of work.

23 **To get the haze off your windshield** that your wipers or washer fluid won't remove, wash the windshield with vinegar, rinse with water, and dry.

24 **If you get stuck in mud or snow,** the best way to get out is to gently accelerate back and forth to produce a rocking motion. Note that 15% tire spin gives you maximum traction; so do not "gun it". Also, do not rock more than a few times, as you are taking a chance of damaging your automatic transmission.

25 **There are many automotive magazines and trade publications that are absolutely free to interested individuals.** All you have to do is ask for them. To locate them, simply go to the library and retrieve a copy of the *Standard Rate and Data.* This publication will list all magazines in circulation. If there is a notation beside that magazine's name that states "Controlled Circulation", it usually means that magazine is free. Just write or call them and ask to be added to their mailing list. Indicate some interest in the magazine's subject matter. Keep in mind that these are not magazines found on the newsstand, but more "insiders" magazines for manufacturers, suppliers, store owners, dealerships, repair centers, etc. They offer extremely valuable information.

26 Almost always **use rebuilt parts rather than buying new ones.** It is much cheaper, and you are getting parts that are, in most cases, just as reliable as new ones. Try to stay with a major brand name as there are some companies producing inferior rebuilt parts.

27 **Compare prices** of replacement parts between the factory dealership (GM, Ford, etc.) and your local auto parts store. They can vary drastically in either one's favor.

28 One of the **simplest and least expensive horsepower gains comes from a tuned free-flowing exhaust**. A set of exhaust headers with a low back-pressure muffler will normally increase horsepower by as much as 20% for just over $200!

29 If you are buying an older used car with an automatic transmission, be careful which one you choose. The **horsepower loss between different transmissions varies dramatically**. The local transmission shop will be able to quote you exact figures on different transmissions and their horsepower "robbing" capabilities. The percentage can range from 10% loss of power all the way up to 35%; although the latter is very rare. Most newer cars are only 4-8%, but watch out for some of the older years.

30 The gear ratio can be changed in direct proportion to the change in tire diameter. If you go up 20% in tire size and want to keep the same shifting points, you will have to go down 20% (actually a 20% increase in numerical numbers) in your gearing. If you choose to change the gear ratio for better fuel economy, **it is much cheaper to purchase used gears from an auto wrecker, because new ring and pinion gears cost a fortune.** I strongly recommend you have the gears installed by a specialist or speed shop. If you shim the pinion or ring gear improperly or incorrectly set the back-lash, you can seize your differential within a few miles of driving.

31 Another great way to get low cost horsepower is to **make sure your engine gets the air it needs to burn fuel**. This can be accomplished by installing a performance air cleaner like ones offered by K&N, or by installing a secondary air cleaner to increase intake volume.

32 Nail polish remover is a great cleaner for small parts. It contains mostly acetone and can **remove tar and bugs from chrome**. Keep in mind that it also removes paint, so don't get it near any.

33 When working on a car and trying to **free a rusted bolt or nut**, use a propane torch to heat it then melt a little candle wax around the head. The wax acts like a lubricant and allows the nut or bolt to be removed easily. As corny as this tip sounds, it works

34 How to **fix an annoying fan belt squeal even after it is adjusted**: if spraying on fan belt dressing only eliminates the problem temporarily, try scuffing the pulley with fine sandpaper.

35 Use aerosol furniture polish for your hard plastic and vinyl interior pieces. It produces a nice shine and keeps dust to a minimum.

36 Philips head screw drivers frequently slip out of the screw groove. Try using a little valve grinding compound on the tip of the screwdriver for tough screws. The gritty compound gives the screw a little more grip preventing you from rounding off the slots in the screw.

37 Automotive hand cleaner works well to **get oil and grease off of ignition wires, vacuum lines and hoses**. Your engine will sparkle.

38 Remember that some metric wrenches work on SAE (English) bolts and vice versa. They aren't exact, but they will often suffice. Try the following possibilities: 1/2 inch = 13mm, 9/16 inch = 14mm, 3/4 inch = 19mm, 13/16 inch = 21mm.

39 Rough idle quick-fix: Many cars with fuel injection can develop a rough idle after 10,000 miles. This may be due to carbon build-up and can be easily eliminated by spraying some carburetor cleaner into the throttle body or air intake while the vehicle is running.

40 Small radiator leak? Stop it with a tablespoon of pepper or some egg white. Although this is a temporary fix, it will get you by until you have a chance to fix the radiator properly.

41 How to find an annoying tick, knock or rattle. Stop by your local autoparts store to purchase an automotive stethoscope (it looks similar to a doctor's one but has a different end). You can use it inside your engine compartment to pinpoint where that tick or rattle is coming from in order to fix it.

42 If you want to **do your own very inexpensive radiator flush,** here's how. Drain the entire system (including the radiator and engine block), refill it with water and 1/2 cup of dishwasher detergent. Run the engine for a few minutes to let the fluid circulate, and then drain completely. Refill and flush again with water to make sure all the detergent is gone. Then refill with coolant. Note: only use dishwasher detergent, other soaps will foam and cause problems.

43 **Remove annoying adhesive residue from your paint** (usually from a sticker you have peeled off) by using WD40 or lighter fluid. Make sure to remove all the fluid after the residue is removed since it can damage the finish of your paint if left in place.

44 If you do your own brake work, **place masking tape over the brake shoes so you don't get grease or oil on them** (which always seems to happen). Then right at the end when everything is in place, remove the tape. (Note: most people forget to remove it, so write a note to yourself and tape it to the steering wheel.)

45 **If you're on the road and your car quits,** most people want to see if the car is getting "spark". Testing this is easy. Take one plug wire off. Take a straightened paperclip or some other convenient piece of metal, and place it inside the plug boot so it touches the metal. Hold the end of the paperclip about 1/4 inch away from a bare metal surface (like an exhaust manifold), and have someone crank the engine over. If you get a spark between the manifold and the paperclip, you are getting spark to the fuel; unless you have a bad plug (very rare).

46 **Never wear jewelry when working on a car.** It can either trap your hand by snagging on a part, or cause an electrical short if you put your hands between a "hot" wire and a grounded part.

47 For people that do "**burn outs**"; there is that rubber build-up on the body that is extremely tough to get off. Next time use a household laundry product called *Spray'n Wash*. It works every time and won't ruin your paint's finish.

48 Studies have shown that **33% of all vehicles on the road have air filters in need of replacement.** This can decrease your fuel economy by up to 10% by providing insufficient air volume to burn fuel dispensed by the injectors. Make sure to check your; it only takes a minute.

49 **Don't rev the engine before turning it off.** This was a common practice for older cars, but it is not necessary for new ones. It can cause excessive wear on the cylinder walls and contaminate the oil with gasoline. You should normally turn an engine off as soon as you stop. Nevertheless, there is an exception to this rule. After a long high-speed trip, let the engine idle for a minute or so before turning it off. This allows the engine to cool, eliminate hot spots, and relieve hot fuel vapors that could cause vapor lock and result in hard starting.

50 **Excessive idling creates engine wear and breeds contaminants in the oil.** Idling is one of the most severe modes of engine operation.

51 **To cool an engine if it is overheating in traffic,** simply put the car in neutral and press down the accelerator slightly to increase the idle. This action increases the coolant flow which should bring the engine temperature down just enough to prevent overheating. If this isn't enough, try rolling down the windows and turning on the heater full blast to dissipate some of the engine heat.

52 **A common problem that baffles most mechanics** is a car that runs fine until it warms up 10-20 miles later and then completely dies. If you let it sit for 30 minutes or so, you can start it up and it will do the same thing all over again. Tell the mechanic that you suspect one or more of the electronic ignition systems is failing after subjected to high temperatures for a period of time. The ignition module, pick-up coil or ignition coil is usually the culprit.

53 **Run the air conditioner at least 10 minutes every week**. This procedure helps avoid costly breakdowns.

54 With a manual transmission, **start the engine in neutral and then engage the clutch**. There is less drag on the engine that way, and it is easier to start (especially in winter months when cold motor oil is very thick).

55 **Many automated car washes do more harm than good**. Rotating brushes, if adjusted for smaller cars, may apply to much pressure to full-sized models scratch the finish. Also, many car washes use recycled water. The salt picked up from previous washings can further rusting (in states experiencing winter salt/sand road conditions). "Hotwax" cycles can damage vinyl tops. New "touchless" car washes use very high pressure spray guns and harsh chemicals to blast away the dirt (and probably part of your wax job). The safest wash is still the old fashioned hand-wash done in the shade.

56 **Don't put sandbags in the trunk of your front wheel drive cars** for extra traction in the winter. The extra weight in the rear actually lessens traction on the front wheels.

CAR NOISES AND RATTLES

As mentioned in the last chapter, use an automotive stethoscope to pinpoint where a noise is coming from so you can fix it.

We will go through the different types of noises — where they come from, and what causes them.

Make careful observations when listening. For example, if there is an under-the-hood noise and it persists when the car is at a complete stop (whether you rev the engine or not), the noise is probably from the engine or related parts. If the noise is occurring when the car is in motion, the problem is probably in the suspension, transmission, rear axle or tires.

Underhood squeals are often from loose or glazed belts. To verify, spray a belt dressing on to see if it stops. Worn bearings in the accessory items can also cause a squeal. To locate it, use the automotive stethoscope or remove the belt to see if the squeal stops.

Clunking on acceleration and deceleration usually indicates worn universal joints.

Underbody roaring, especially if it gets louder on acceleration, can be caused by a small hole in the exhaust. The smallest hole can make a real racket. Look for holes or broken clamps which have allowed pipe joints to separate.

Clunking when braking may indicate loose brake calipers, defective shock absorbers or loose suspension components.

Engine noises are the biggest area of complaint. A "tick" or "pinging" sound from the engine is actually the gas <u>exploding</u> in the combustion chamber instead of burning. This is called detonation. It is most common during acceleration and can cause serious damage after a while. If it occurs, try using a higher octane gas. If this does not cure the problem, have your mechanic check the ignition timing, carbon build-up, and the EGR valve.

A clicking sound for a short time after the engine is started is **normal.** It takes a minute for the oil to flow to the hydraulic lifters. However, if the ticking continues, the oil may be low or the lifters may need servicing.

Hissing noises indicate an air or vacuum leak. It is usually a disconnected or damaged hose. This is easy to trace with a stethoscope.

Vibrations in the floor or the seat when traveling over 35 mph can be coming from the drive shaft (rear wheel drive cars), rear axle, rear tires or unbalanced brake drums. If the vibration only happens at certain high speeds, it is most often a tire imbalance. An inexpensive tire balance should fix the problem.

Under-body whine, especially when accelerating or decelerating, is predominantly a rear axle or front drive unit problem.

A common problem is dash rattle. There is an **easy fix** to this very annoying, irritating problem. Move your hand over the dash applying pressure to see when the rattle stops. When you find that area, first try to tighten the retaining screws. If this doesn't work, loosen the part and slip in a sheet of rubber as an insulator. Then re-tighten the part down.

With wind noises, faulty weather stripping is usually the culprit. To pinpoint it, just use masking tape to cover up the suspected areas and gradually remove sections of the tape until the noise re-occurs. Either replace the bad weather stripping, re-adjust the window, or use silicone to fill in the area. A broken section of grill may also cause a wind noise.

THE ALMIGHTY TUNE-UP RIP-OFFS

Engine tune-ups have largely become <u>an</u> <u>over</u> <u>priced</u> <u>rip</u> <u>off</u>. Did you know that if you own a car built in the mid-to-late 1980's it probably does not require a tune up?

You must be thinking I'm crazy, "A car not requiring a tune up? Ridiculous"! Well, hear me out.

ALMOST EVERY CAR BUILT NOW IS RUN BY A COMPUTER AND DOES NOT NEED THE TUNE UP THAT WE ARE ACCUSTOMED TO PAYING FOR

But old habits die hard, so we are suckered into it. I call it "the grandfather syndrome". What a waste of your money.

In earlier years, cars had distributors, carburetors, etc. These had to be tuned, maintained and adjusted periodically. This is no longer the case. There are no more distributor caps with points or condensers and no more carburetors to adjust. The cars are now fuel-injected with high performance electronic ignition and fuel injection systems all controlled by a computer that monitors the engine's performance.

The computer actually adjusts the necessary components to maximize fuel efficiency, engine performance and exhaust emissions. So what is left to "tune-up", you ask? That is a good question.

Generally, the only items a car needs are new spark plugs, PVC valve, and air/fuel filters every 30,000 miles or so. This is specified in your owners manual, but I know how many of us actually *read* them. This is not a tune-up, just regular maintenance.

QUICK STOP TUNE-UP SHOPS HAVE BEEN POPPING UP EVERYWHERE TO TAKE ADVANTAGE OF THE CUSTOMER'S LACK OF KNOWLEDGE REGARDING TUNE-UPS

If you check the fine print at these shops (or any shop that charges high prices for "tune ups"), you will notice other than replacing the spark plugs and maybe a few filters, the word "check" is found everywhere (e.g. check wires, check emission hoses, check this, check that). Just lots of "checks", not a whole lot of "tuning up" your car. And most likely, the majority of these checks are not done so the profits run even higher for the shop.

If you want to verify that your car does not need a tune up, just look at your emissions control sticker in the engine compartment. Most stickers on cars built in the mid to late 1980's will say "no idle mixture, idle speed, or ignition timing adjustments are possible". <u>There goes your tune-up!</u>

If your car is not running well, <u>do not ask for a tune-up</u>, ask for a **diagnostic checkup**. If your car is getting poor fuel mileage, again, do not ask for a tune-up. Poor fuel economy could be caused by many things. A tune-up is where a bunch of parts are replaced and checked **in the hope** that your car will run better. You want to locate the problem and fix it permanently. This is what the computer is for! With a diagnostics check-up, the mechanic reads codes in the computer to find out the problem is in order to solve it immediately. That is why we have all this new technology in cars!

Bad gas can also make you think you need a "tune-up". Bad gas is gas that either contains some water, general contaminants or is just plainly "old gas". If you have water in the gas there are additives you can buy at any auto parts store to remedy the problem.

That brings to mind another great tip...

NEVER PURCHASE GAS FROM A STATION WHILE THE TANKER TRUCK IS FILLING THE STATION'S STORAGE TANKS

When they fill up the station's tanks, the dirt and contaminants from the bottom of the tank get stirred up into some of the gas you may pump right into your car.

One of my favorite gimmicks is the overpriced fuel injector cleaner. Sorry to break the news to you, but similar injector cleaning power is in almost every tank of gas you purchase.

That's right. Since the late 80's, when most car manufacturers where switching from carburation to fuel injection, major gas companies have had to put these additives into their gas to prevent carbon build-up on the injectors and clogging problems. When the gas companies in their T.V. commercials say the car is running cleaner because of their gas, **it is true**.

All these injector cleaners are just concentrated versions of the cleaners already in your gas. You <u>should not</u> be using them with every few tanks of gas (as they might suggest at $4.00 a bottle). They are only necessary if you have dirty or clogged injectors. They are the cheap alternative that might fix the problem before you go and spend the money on an expensive injector purge ($75.00).

OK, let's go over some easily overlooked solutions to common problems.

If the car seems to surge or hesitate and you are experiencing high oil consumption, check the PCV valve before you ask for a tune up. Both of these are symptoms of a bad or plugged PCV valve. (Keep in mind not every engine is equipped with a PCV valve.)

Engines that stall without warning usually have an electrical problem; not a performance problem. Have the mechanic look for weak ground connections or worn wire insulation causing a short.

An engine that lacks power is usually thought of as an engine in need of a tune-up. This is <u>far</u> from the truth. As I mentioned before, it could be a multitude of problems. A commonly overlooked cause is a crushed exhaust pipe or clogged muffler. This can seriously dampen engine performance.

The "Great Mileage Scam" is a common trick used by mechanics. Even reputable chain stores are getting away with this. After you get your tune-up you notice the great mileage you are getting from your car. You thinking "Wow, what a great job that shop did, I am definitely going there again". They <u>did not</u> work any miracles, all they did was over inflate the tires 5 pounds. This gives the tires less rolling resistance and therefore better fuel economy (and a rougher ride because of the harder tires). So if your car's ride seems a little hard after you have had a tune up, check the tire pressure.

As you know, carbureted engines do need tune-ups, which can increase fuel mileage an average of 11%. Nevertheless, if you have a carbureted engine and you are getting it tuned-up, there is a cover-up that happens **all the time.**

On older cars, many times the mechanic will not be able to get the car running smoothly by using the exact manufacturers settings and staying within emission controls. To cover this up, he may make some of his own "hot rod" adjustments. Two of the easiest ways to get more power and make an engine run smoother is to either advance the timing a few degrees or richen up the carburetor mixture. The problem is you probably wouldn't realize something is wrong until you try to get your car smog tested (and probably fail) or noticed the drop in fuel economy.

Also, one last tip for carbureted engines. Many times mechanics automatically replace distributor cap, rotor, coil, ignition wires and possibly the ignition coil. This is not necessary, so do not let them take advantage of you. Most of these items are good for 50,000 miles, they only need to be <u>checked</u> in a tune-up. Many mechanics will recommend to replace them anyway as "preventative maintenance" or an "insurance policy" for a trouble free car. To do so would be wasting your money: **only replace the parts that are bad.**

There are many quick stop shops that aggressively market air filter and PVC valves during an oil change or whatever. Usually they receive a commission for every extra part they sell you. Don't replace these more often than what the manufacturer recommends. Unless you drive in very dusty environment, you are just wasting your money.

UNLESS YOU ARE DRIVING A HIGH PERFORMANCE AUTOMOBILE, PROFESSIONAL FUEL INJECTOR CLEANINGS ARE ALMOST ALWAYS A WASTE OF MONEY

Nevertheless, many repair shops recommend this as a solution to many performance problems or as a requirement of a regular maintenance tune-up. As you are aware, cleaning agents are present in every tank of gas we buy. There is an occasional situation where an injector may get clogged and the additives in our gas or a concentrated injector cleaner won't clear it. In this case, it is only necessary to clean one injector, *not the entire set*. A good mechanic will be able to determine very quickly that a clogged injector is the problem.

Many consumers are also talked into a tune-up after a battery replacement. The computer monitors your engine's performance and adjusts the fuel delivery to its needs. This information is kept in the computer's memory until you disconnect the battery. Once the battery is disconnected all this information is lost from memory and the computer goes back to standard settings. It takes a few trips around the block for the computer to re-learn your car's needs and adjust to them. So for the first few minutes the car may run poorly. Do not let the mechanic talk you into a tune-up, when the computer would have corrected itself.

If you can stay around to monitor the repair, the chances of getting ripped off decreases rapidly. Your presence usually keeps mechanics on their toes.

The best part about tune-ups is that if your car is still under its emission warranty, you **should not have to pay for any diagnosis or repairs** for a poorly run car because most of those components are covered under that warranty. The process of how to do this is completely covered in the "Getting Free Repairs After Your Warranty Has Expired" chapter.

HOW TO FIX INTERMITTENT
PERFORMANCE PROBLEMS IN MINUTES

This has happened to all of us. An engine problem acts up now and then. You take it to the repair shop and the problem disappears when you are trying to show the mechanic what is wrong. The understanding mechanic tells you he can't fix what is not there, "come back when it happens again".

The good news is that there are a couple of tricks to fix this problem.

Most intermittent problems are caused by wiring or an electrical connection malfunction. The problem may happen when the car gets hot and the connection goes bad, or it may happen when you hit the accelerator when the cruise control is on causing the throttle linkage to rub against a connection and short it out. The possibilities are endless. Many of these problems do not set "trouble codes" in the computer for the technician to retrieve.

Unfortunately, the mechanics are so used to removing and replacing parts, many don't get back to basics. If they can't find a trouble code in the computer to help them pinpoint the problem, they express their regret and tell you to come back when it happens again. The first thing that you should do is to ask the mechanic to duplicate the situation. For example, say the car is really warmed up and the throttle is at half way when the problem starts. Then you should ask him to wiggle every wire and connection he can think of. Start tapping the sensors and relays to see if the disturbance induces the problem to occur. Many times this will induce the problem by starting a short, or separating an electrical connection, etc. If this does not work, move to plan B.

Plan B is called a computer "snapshot" or snapshot test. This is where a device called a scanner is hooked to your car computer (or ECM as they call it). You drive around normally with this device activated. The scanner is set to trigger when it sees something abnormal. The scanner takes a "snapshot" of the data the computer is generating just before, during and after the problem arises. This information can be retrieved by the mechanic to pinpoint the problem. It is an ingenious device that is relatively inexpensive, but many repair shops do not have them because most of their work is general repairs not diagnostics (especially rare problems).

I also want to cover a common rip-off occurring in a rough running carbureted car (most newer cars will not have this problem).

Does your car have these symptoms:

1. Engine hesitates or stalls when it is cold

2. Loss of power and fuel economy

3. Erratic idle speed

4. Car "pings" even though you are using the proper octane level gas

These symptoms can indicate **carbon build-up**. Carbureted cars tend to experience carbon build-up because they have to run rich due to the fact that the cylinders closest to the carburetor will run richer than those furthest (due to the length of the intake manifold).

THOUSANDS OF CUSTOMERS ARE SOLD USELESS TUNE-UPS TO CORRECT THIS PROBLEM

You don't need one.

Carbon tends to accumulate on top of the pistons and on the underside of the engine intake valves.

Certain models of vehicles are more susceptible to carbon build-up. Generally, these are small displacement engines designed for high performance. Among some of these are BMW, Audi, Volkswagen and Porsche.

The carbon build-up can glow red hot and ignite incoming fuel into the combustion chamber. This effectively advances the ignition timing so you may get detonation.

There are ways to reduce this shown in the "Almighty Tune-up Rip-offs" section. You might also want to try a tank of premium grade gas from a major gas company before you get any major servicing done to your intake valves or fuel injectors. Most of the time, they put more detergents into this grade and that <u>could</u> solve your problem. Pour a can of carbon cleaner in your gas tank to assist the detergents in the gas. This cleaner can be found at any auto parts store.

As a maintenance procedure, I like to fill up my tank with a good premium gas once in a while for the extra cleaning capabilities. However, I might consider asking the gas attendant or field representative what the differences are in his grades of gas. Some companies get away with adding only a few extra additives to the premium grade gases and then marking them up for more profit. That's why I recommend to stay with a national brand as their gas content is generally controlled and regulated.

Another idea is to call your local BMW dealership. State you are aware older BMWs are more prone to carbon build-up and some gases are more suitable for them. Ask him to recommend a gas company he thinks has the cleanest fuel. Some gas companies actually advertise that their gas is recommended for European built cars such as BMW, Porsche and Audi.

If you suspect carbon build-up on your intake valves, most good repair shops have a baroscope. This fiber optic device allows the mechanics to view the inside of the engine. It is a good idea to verify that is your problem before you authorize the mechanic to do an expensive physical removal of carbon build-up.

Listen up folks, on the next page there is something you will never see anywhere. As far as I know, this is the first time it has been published. If you ask a mechanic what causes engine "pinging" or "knocking" — he will most likely tell you detonation or pre-ignition is the cause. If you ask him what causes detonation or pre-ignition, he will probably say, "low octane gas". If you ask him why? He will probably say, "I don't know".

Since engine "pinging" is so common, you should understand what it means. I am going to tell you why the mechanic is not necessarily right.

Actually detonation and pre-ignition are completely different. Depending on the design and limits of your engine...,

A LITTLE PRE-IGNITION MAY NOT BE DANGEROUS; BUT DETONATION IS A KILLER!

Pre-ignition is the main cause of detonation, but the two items are separate issues.

Pre-ignition is just what it sounds — the fuel is ignited before it is supposed to be. This can be caused by glowing red hot carbon deposits, sharp edges in the combustion chamber creating a hot spot, advanced timing, or by spark plugs that become too hot and ignite the fuel too early.

Normally, the following happens in a proper running engine. The piston moves up the combustion chamber towards the top where the fuel is ignited just slightly before the piston reaches the top (known as "top-dead-center"). The burning/expansion of the fuel forces the piston down to give you "power". When you have pre-ignition, the fuel is ignited long before the piston reaches the top so that the piston is now compressing the burning fuel while still on the up-stroke.

This process works against the normal operation of the engine and generates excessive heat and pressure inside the combustion chamber while at the same time **robbing** your engine of its normal power. The severity of the problem lies in how soon the fuel is ignited before its intended time. As it gets more severe, it causes another problem called *detonation*, which we will get into next.

In any case, pre-ignition is definitely not good for your engine.

The next step to understand is the octane rating of gasoline. Gasoline normally burns at a rate of about one hundred feet per second. In other words, if I pour a trail of gas on the ground that was 100 feet long and lit a match at one end, it would take about one second to reach the other end. This controlled rate of burn is what gives the PUSH (not bang) that pushes the pistons to give your engine power. However, there is a funny thing about gasoline. If the combination of heat and pressure become to high, the gasoline breaks down at a molecular level and no longer burns at 100 ft/sec, but instead

BURNS AT 7,000 FEET PER SECOND!
— LITERALLY AN EXPLOSION.

This is known as detonation.

Without getting into the chemistry involved, it is suffice to say that octane rating is a number which represents the amount of heat and .pressure the gasoline will take before the flame front changes from a controlled burn to an explosion; or "detonation".

The higher the number, the more heat and pressure the gas can take. This is why high compression engines need higher octane fuel. They are more efficient, but also operate under higher temperatures and pressure.

Are you still with me through all this technical babble? Hang on and let's continue with the real bad boy on the block; "detonation".

Remember when I talked about pre-ignition? I said that the fuel was ignited while the piston was still moving upward on the up-stroke (or called the compression stroke). Think about this. We are no longer compressing just the fuel/air mixture, but also working against hot, expanding, burning gasoline. This creates excessive heat and pressure. Remember that gasoline detonates under a combination of heat and pressure.

We have the piston moving upward on the compression stroke and something causes the air/fuel mixture to ignite before its time. The temperature and pressure rise and suddenly the gasoline detonates. So you say, "big deal, the flame front moved from 100 to 7,000 ft/sec." Well, it is a big deal! When the fuel/air mixture burned at 100 ft/second, that energy is released over a period of time that gave the piston its pushing action. At 7,000 ft/sec, that energy is released *instantaneously and there* *are humungous forces at work. When the gasoline goes from a burn to an explosion (detonation), the piston is **slammed down** to the bottom and all the bearings in the piston connecting rods and crankshaft are pounded — giving you the knocking sound. This generally happens only when you are "under load" such as acceleration or high speeds. This is due to the fact that pressure increases in the combustion chamber as the "load" on the engine increases.*

In extreme situations, if detonation occurs while the piston still has a ways to go before it reaches the top, you won't believe the damage it can do within seconds. You would either throw a connecting rod through the side of your engine or melt a hole through the top of your piston. Either way, **you are talking about thousands of dollars in damage**.

"Pinging" is generally caused by light to medium detonation. For example, when the piston is on its way back down and a portion of the fuel has been burned, if the left over fuel is detonated, there is not enough energy left to make the hard "knock", but still enough to give you a "ping".

How does the use of higher octane fuel sometimes fix this problem?

As mentioned previously, the octane rating is a combination between pressure and heat of where the fuel's flame front jumps to 7,000 ft/sec. If you have a higher octane fuel, it will take more pressure before it begins to explode. Therefore you would still have the pre-ignition but reduced chances of detonation.

Gasoline loses its octane rating as it ages. If you get old or bad gas with a low octane, it can detonate in a normally good working engine. If your car is running fine one day and then starts knocking or pinging just after you fill-up, be suspicious of that tank of gas. You don't have to drain that gas unless it is really severe. Just drive your car gently until you're down to a half a tank, then fill it up with the highest octane gas you can find. Or, a second, easier solution is to buy a can of octane booster at any auto parts store.

GET FREE REPAIRS AFTER YOUR WARRANTY HAS EXPIRED

Remember, unless you ask if something is covered under warranty, the information will not usually be volunteered.

Before I show you how to get free repairs, we should go over some important information.

If you buy a car from dealer "A" and want warranty work from dealer "B", dealer "B" will resent that you didn't buy the car from him and you may have some problems. By law, every dealership has to provide warranty service no matter where you bought the car. However, they can really give you the run around if they wish. They could stall you by claiming there is no appointment available for weeks, or even if your car does get into the shop, it could sit for days before work actually commences, therefore deterring you from going there again.

There is a way to improve the relationship between you and dealer "B". Speak to the service manager and explain that you want him to do all the servicing work to your car, including all paid maintenance work and repairs, because you are not happy with the service at dealer "A". When you ask for warranty work, also ask for some inexpensive job like an oil change.

Before we discuss how to get free repairs after your warranty expires, I am going to show you how many ways to get free repairs you would normally pay for while your car is still under warranty.

MANY OF THE COMPONENTS YOU USUALLY PAY TO HAVE REPAIRED ARE COVERED UNDER YOUR WARRANTY

To give you the perfect example, when most customers come in and complain of a poor running engine they are sold a tune-up. Don't pay for this — the diagnostics and repair of a poor running engine are covered under your five year/50,000 mile warranty.* **Think emission warranty, not tune-ups.**

---

* *warranty period may vary depending on car manufacturer and model year.*

Many consumers are charged for things like new PCV valves, ignition wires, fuel injectors, etc. These should all be <u>free</u> under your warranty, but most customers pay for them. You will be surprised at how many parts are covered under most warranties. Here are a few: PCV valve, intake manifold, oxygen sensor, ignition wires and distributor, EGR valve, turbochargers, catalytic converter, fuel injectors, exhaust manifold, and all related hoses and wires. And there are many more parts covered under your 2 year, 24,000 mile* performance warranty.

It is not always easy to get repairs done under the emissions warranty. Independent shops do not have the authority to do warranty work for the manufacturer. Therefore, if you are getting your car repaired and something is covered under warranty...

THEY ARE LIKELY TO CHARGE YOU FOR THE REPAIR

Although dealerships do get paid for warranty work by the manufacturer, it pays substantially less than non-warranty work. Proving defective workmanship on emission components is difficult, so they are taking the risk that the warranty claim may be completely rejected by the car manufacturer and they may have to end up absorbing the cost. So the dealer has incentive to try and make you pay for emissions work.

Sometimes a customer will get frustrated with a particular problem the dealership hasn't been able to fix properly under warranty. After taking the car to the dealership a few times, they get fed up and pay for an independent mechanic to look at it. Do not do this. It is the responsibility of the manufacturer to fix the problem. Do not pay money out of <u>your</u> pocket to do so. Just contact the manufacturers district (or zone) representative and you should get results.

IF YOU EVER FAIL AN EMISSIONS TEST WHILE UNDER THE WARRANTY PERIOD, THERE IS A GOOD CHANCE THE REPAIRS ARE COVERED FREE UNDER YOUR WARRANTY

Don't expect the independent repair shop that did the test to tell you this. He wants to charge you for those repairs.

---

* *warranty period may vary depending on car manufacturer and model year.*

If your engine burns too much oil, do not settle for the excuse that for every 1,000 miles the car burns one quart of oil. **This is hogwash with newer cars. Any car that burns more that one quart of oil per 2,000 miles is considered high oil consumption.**

High oil consumption can be a very serious problem. It can be caused by bad piston rings, valves stem seals or cylinder walls. Nevertheless, most car manufacturers are not concerned about high oil consumption. If you cannot get the problem resolved under warranty at the local dealership, try contacting the district service manager then the car manufacturer's zone representative. If you get no satisfaction with these people then there is one last resort which almost always works.

Write a letter to the manufacturer's zone office explaining that high oil consumption contaminates the oxygen sensor. When this part becomes contaminated, the car's computer can't correctly control the fuel mixture. This increases emission. State you are aware of the correlation of high oil consumption and increased emissions. Mention that you are considering contacting the Environmental Protection Agency (EPA), but will not do so until they have replied. If there is no response, contact the EPA, Warranty Complaints, Washington, DC 20460, (202) 382-2640. If it ever gets this far, you can bet the problem will be resolved the instant the EPA gets involved.

Another example of free repairs done under warranty is the common rotten egg smell some new car owners get from their exhaust. The catalytic converter is usually the cause of the problem since the exhaust odor affects air quality which is tightly controlled by federal law. You can get a new catalytic converter free of charge under your emissions warranty.

You paid for your warranty when you bought the car, since it is factored into the price of any new car. The best way to take full advantage of your warranty is to have an independent mechanic do a complete pre-expiration inspection of your car. It is a mistake to have the dealership do this because they can let a few things slide, in hope that you will pay for the repair after the warranty has expired and the problem has worsened. Most dealers don't like doing warranty work and may not judge your car fairly.

THE IDEA IS TO LOCATE FAILING PARTS
OR MALFUNCTIONS BEFORE THE WARRANTY EXPIRES

The cost of this inspection should be about $50. It is <u>critical</u> that the mechanic documents everything he finds. Bring that to the dealership and have the repairs done free before the warranty expires.

Important: Keep in mind that most parts do not fail instantaneously, but deteriorate. These parts will operate at a substandard level for a while before they break down completely. This is what the mechanic should be looking for when he does his inspection.

Make sure to have him check the computer "codes". The computer monitors the engine all the time. Any time something is out-of-the-ordinary, it stores a code of where the problem lies. If the problem is significant enough, your "service engine soon" light comes on the dashboard. Make sure he has recorded all of these codes on your repair order, it could point out a possible problem. Other things he should check are fluid leaks (including engine oil), steering and suspension linkages, warped brake rotors or drums, engine performance (especially engine "pinging"), charging system and all belts and hoses. These all should be covered under your warranty if not up to snuff.

Now, for the good stuff...

TO GET FREE REPAIRS AFTER YOUR WARRANTY HAS
EXPIRED, IT IS <u>IMPERATIVE</u> THAT YOU KEEP ALL YOUR
REPAIR BILLS FROM THE TIME YOU BUY YOUR CAR

It doesn't matter if they couldn't find the source of your problem; still keep the receipt showing your specific complaint and what tests they did. This will help you immensely.

Make sure that when you go to get repair work done, the repair order describes the <u>exact</u> problem and the <u>exact</u> test results they found (or what they couldn't find). It is important to be armed with complaints you may have made before the warranty's expiration. If a problem arises and it is related to a complaint you have been making, you can ask for warranty work to be done even though your warranty is expired, on the grounds that it was a problem when the car <u>was</u> under warranty and was never fixed properly. Without the report order to prove this specific problem, you would just be wasting your time.

There are also what are called **"Secret Warranties"** or **"Goodwill Adjustments"**. These refer to a warranty that is not publicly announced and/or may cover repairs that are not normally covered under warranty.

In other words, **you can get a problem fixed even though your car is not under warranty anymore**. The only disadvantage to this process is that you only get it if you complain and protest enough. If you are a timid person, you may be paying for repairs others are getting free.

HOW DO YOU FIND OUT IF YOUR CAR'S PROBLEM IS COVERED UNDER A SECRET WARRANTY?

That's easy!

Just call your car manufacturer's customer service department (the phone number is in your owner's manual). Describe your problem and ask if there is a "policy adjustment provision" covering this. Dealers and manufacturers <u>do</u> <u>not</u> <u>acknowledge</u> the existence of "secret warranties", however, they do recognize policy adjustment. These adjustments are basically an extension of warranty coverage on a case-by-case basis.

There is another tell-tale sign there may be a secret warranty on your particular car's problem. Ask the service manager if there is a technical service bulletin on this repair. If so, there is a good chance it is covered under a policy adjustment.

I had a few friends who owned Pontiac Fieros. One got a set of <u>free</u> rear tires because the factory miscalculated the toe-in setting of the rear alignment and caused excessive tire wear.

CUSTOMER ASSISTANCE NUMBERS.

MANUFACTURER	PHONE NO	MANUFACTURER	PHONE NO	MANUFACTURER	PHONE NO
Ford	(800)392-3673	Mercedes-Benz	(800)222-0100	Ford Trucks	(800)392-3673
Acura	(800)382-2238	Mercury	(800)392-3673	Alfa Romeo	(800)225-1575
GEO	(800)222-1020	Mitsubishi	(800)222-0037	Aston Martin	(800)813-0296
GMC Truck	(800)462-8782	AM General	(800)732-5493	Nissan	(800)647-7261
Audi	(800)822-2834	Hyundai	(800)633-5151	Oldsmobile	(800)442-6537
Bentley	(800)777-6923	Infiniti	(800)662-6200	Plymouth	(800)992-1997
BMW	(800)831-1117	Isuzu	(800)255-6727	Pontiac	(800)762-2737
Bugatti	(800)245-6887	Jaguar	(800)818-8100	Porsche	(800)545-8039
Buick	(800)521-7300	Jeep	(800)992-1997	Rolls-Royce	(800)777-6923
Cadillac	(800)458-8006	KIA	(800)333-4542	Saab	(800)955-9007
Chevrolet	(800)222-1020	Lamborghini	(800)882-5872	Saturn	(800)553-6000
Chrysler	(800)992-1997	Land Rover	(800)637-6837	Subaru	(800)782-2783
Dodge	(800)992-1997	Lexus	(800)255-3987	Suzuki	(800)934-0934
Dodge Trucks	(800)992-1997	Lincoln	(800)392-3673	Toyota	(800)331-4331
Eagle	(800)992-1997	Lotus	(800)992-1997	Volkswagen	(800)822-8987

This was published in a technical bulletin and he protested that it should be covered by GM because it was their fault. There you have it: a "policy adjustment".

Another friend that owned a Fiero received a free clutch because the car had some weak components. After enough complaining, the $600 repair was reimbursed by GM. Again, this clutch problem was described in a technical service bulletin.

When getting a "policy adjustment", one way to approach the situation (if you do not get anywhere with the service manager) is to write the manufacturer's zone office stating the date and number of the bulletin. Note that you are aware of the problem and feel it should be covered at no charge as it was an inherent design flaw of the car when you bought it.

To get copies of the service bulletins, call (202) 366-2768 and ask for the technical reference library. This library will print out a list of all the bulletins on file. You just select the ones you are interested in and order them. The service manager of your dealership should have all of these on file if you wish to get them from him instead.

Sometimes the manufacturer will give you an excuse about why they cannot cover your claim, even though it seems evident to you that they are responsible and should cover it in a policy adjustment.

THIS IS JUST A SMOKE SCREEN TO WEED OUT THE LIARS, FALSE CLAIMS AND PEOPLE LOOKING FOR A "FREE RIDE"!

If you feel your claim is justified, stick to it and be persistent. Have documented evidence to back up your claim and think logically. Raising a fuss will get you nowhere.

If it ever comes to the point where you are negotiating for free repairs, make sure to always remember to remind them of the benefits to them. An example: tell them you were considering buying another car of the same make because you have been happy with this one, however, you may have to re-evaluate that situation if you cannot get good service. You might point out your past loyalty to the car line. You may also use tactics like saying you feel the car is unsafe. If your car had a fuel or ignition problem, you might state you are scared that if the car stalls in an intersection it may cause a fatal accident. Factory personnel are trained to spot potential product liability litigation in the making. So the "safety angle" could be used to your advantage.

It is important that you **do not** show intent to never buy this product again. Why should they spend money to satisfy you if you never intend to purchase a product from them again? To them, you're a lost customer.

Never threaten with a law suit! It is good to lightly hint about litigation, but threatening a law suit only works against you. First, the manufacturer wants to "save face" and not be pushed around by one customer. If you back them into a corner, they will fight. Also, it indicates that you are so upset that even spending the money to rectify the problem is probably pointless because they have already lost you as a future customer.

Whenever you are negotiating for warranty work, make sure you are firm and confident, never annoying, irate or hostile. Doing this usually causes them to do the same.

If the car has been used for anything but its intended purpose, the warranty is void. This includes such things as going off-road, racing and modifying the fuel delivery system or emissions equipment.

In the next chapter, I will show you how good dealerships cheat the warranty system to give good warranty service to their customer. It is discussed in that chapter because a dealership service department and how they handle warranty repairs is the most important factor influencing where to buy your new car.

As a final note, I have a tip on getting **free suspension repairs from hitting potholes.** It has nothing to do with the warranty, but did you know that many times suspension or front end damage resulting from hitting a pothole can be claimed under the collision portion of your insurance policy?

WHY CAR DEALERS DON'T WANT TO DO WARRANTY WORK AND HOW GOOD DEALERS BEAT THE SYSTEM!

As I mentioned before, doing warranty work is a real hassle for the dealer. They not only get paid much less per hour, but they must tag and retain the defective part until a factory representative can inspect it and certify that it is defective. This costs time and money.

It will cost even more money if the factory representative rejects the warranty claim. If he feels the part is not defective and there has been an improper diagnostic by the mechanic, it can lead to an argument between the manager and the factory representative. Again, more time and money wasted.

As mentioned before, the easy way to avoid all of this is for the dealer to give you excuses long enough for the warranty to expire. Once the warranty expires, the mechanic finds a problem with the part and replaces it at your expense. But unlike the low warranty wages and parts the factory would pay for, the dealership makes about 40% more profit servicing your car at the retail prices. When getting repairs done under warranty, demand results if you are getting flimsy excuses or explanations.

For most warranty repairs, the factory pays a fixed amount of time for the repair as stated by the warranty guide manual and a lower fixed labor rate too. For example, a factory guide will allow one hour for labor to be paid by the factory.

When a regular customer pays for a repair, you are charged the retail labor rate and the time allotted is sometimes taken from a much more generous and liberal independent labor guide manual.

Another problem for the dealers is although the unsuspecting customer might accept getting charged again and again for repairs due to incorrect diagnosis rather than fixing the problem right the first time, the manufacturer will not accept this. They refuse to pay for the dealer's incompetence and lack of automotive knowledge. In other words, the dealer can not get away with the outrageous charges they sometimes bill customers with.

MANY CAR DEALERSHIPS TEND TO COMPLETELY DISMISS ALL THE WARRANTY REPAIRS POSSIBLE...

They concentrate on selling cars and not servicing them. You would think the car manufacturer would revoke their franchise license when they are giving lousy service to their customers (and potential repeat car buyers). Under current law it is very difficult to cancel their franchise if the dealer is selling a large quantity of cars.

However, **there is good news**. Good dealers can beat the warranty system and benefit all their customers. This is done generally through warranty padded claims and some car manufacturer's treatment of certain dealers better (and in conjunction, you better).

Say your five year warranty has expired four months ago, and you now have a bad brake caliper. You're feeling that this part was failing while the warranty was in effect, but didn't actually fail completely until it had expired. The service manager may sympathize with you because you make regular visits and are a good customer. He may replace your brake caliper and claim a warranty repair under another customer's car that is still under warranty, therefore fixing your car for free.

Another customer that is in for regular repair or warranty repairs will be told that another problem was found in this brake caliper and the part was replaced under warranty. In fact, this part was never replaced, but the money collected from the factory either...

PAYS FOR LEGITIMATE REPAIRS ON A CAR WHEN THE WARRANTY HAS JUST EXPIRED,
OR
GOES DIRECTLY IN THE DEALER'S BACK POCKET TO SUBSIDIZE HEAVY DISCOUNTING ON NEW CAR SALES

If the manager can make $200 in a fake warranty claim, he can lower the price of a new car by $200 more and beat the competition.

He can also repair a few cars on which the warranty has just expired for free, therefore making his customers happy and creating repeat customers. **It makes good business sense**.

The only concern is that if a dealership is this dishonest with the factory, it may be crooked with you, too, at some point.

In many high priced warranty claims, a factory inspection representative is required to inspect a customer's vehicle before warranty work is started. If the service manager has a good reputation with the factory inspection representative, the factory rep may trust the service manager to do warranty repairs on his own initiative. This is a great benefit to you because now you don't have to leave your car at the dealership for a few days while the representative comes by to inspect it. Also, if you are a good customer, the local manager may sway to your side if deciding whether your paint was actually defective or was really destroyed by industrial fallout (the factory representative would not let this "slide".

HOW TO EASILY PASS THE SMOG TEST AND HOW THEY RIP YOU OFF WITHOUT YOU KNOWING

If you don't have mandatory emission (smog) checks in your state yet, **you will soon.** The federal government is being pressured to support this initiative because of acid rain, the destruction of our ozone layer, and the greenhouse effect. Because this is becoming a mandatory repair service, it is prone to dishonesty.

The test is divided into two sections, the visual inspection and the actual emissions test. The visual inspection is where all the problems are.

Most customers are misled after the visual inspection. The technician may come back and tell you that you need a new air cleaner, PCV valve and a couple of vacuum hoses. How does he know this? **He hasn't even run it through the emissions test yet!** Most consumers think these recommendations are essential to the test and **pay for the repairs, even before the test is run**.

Other technicians may not make recommendations outright, but lead you into it by saying things like "I don't know about the air filter", You may reply, "Do you think I should replace it"? His answer will always be "Yes, it is a really good idea".

If you have recently had your car serviced and they made these types of recommendations, I would be suspicious.

Don't ever let the mechanic lean in under your hood and touch <u>anything</u>, he has no reason to do so. He is only justified in touching anything when the actual test is being performed. Some unscrupulous mechanics will actually sabotage the vehicle by disconnecting a vacuum hose or something similar.

With this aside, there are many little tricks to help you pass your smog test.

Volvo is another example of a car that is overpriced and over-rated. A good quality car, but marketed to Yuppies that focus on the image not the value.

If you are interested about saving money and aren't concerned about brand name recognition, consider buying a cheaper "twin". This is where you will find two identical cars made by the same manufacturer but marketed under different names. For example, Mitsubishi Eclipse and Plymouth Laser are *the same car*, but the Mitsubishi is over a thousand dollars more expensive.

If you want to get reviews on the cars you are considering pur-chasing, *Motor Trend* and *Car and Driver* magazines publish yearly buyer's guides with specs and opinions on the vehicles. If you are a member of the American Automobile Association (AAA), they publish reviews of many of the cars available and you can get them free. Just call the office.

Do realize that Japanese cars hold a higher resale value because of their perceived higher quality? But they are also more ex-pensive initially and much more expensive for repairs.

When deciding on a car, make sure you are aware of the repair costs...;

MANY CARS HAVE **VERY** DIFFERENT REPAIR COSTS THAT CAN PUSH YOUR YEARLY REPAIR BILL THROUGH THE CEILING.

For example, a Mazda is a good car, but a complete rear brake job on some models will run you around $800 (most domestic cars would cost around $250).

Another consideration is how readily available the parts are for your car. If you buy an import, it can be harder or take longer to find parts and be a hassle if you have an urgent repair. This can be a serious consideration. If your area has an abundance of import parts you are fine, but if you travel a lot, you may not find the same abundance. Many foreign car owners have experienced the unpleasantness of breaking down in a remote area only to find out the nearest qualified service center is 50 miles away.

If you are not set on a color or certain options, you might also want to consider buying what are the most popular colors and options. It will make your car much easier to sell a few years from now.

BE WARY OF "TOO GOOD TO BE TRUE" ADVERTISING. THERE IS ALWAYS A CATCH

Have you read the advertisements, "Buy $1 over invoice", or "$1,000 below invoice for last years' models". They are absolutely true. **However,** it will be only for current dealers stock and many times you <u>will</u> <u>have</u> to buy their high priced dealer installed options and extras like rustproofing, etc. Somewhere it will probably say that the dealer retains all rebates and incentives. **This can amount to hundreds of dollars.**

How about "Save $5,000 on a new Honda". If you read the fine print, it will most likely apply to just one vehicle on the lot; the rest are sold at full price. And who is to know the strings that are attached to that price? So don't be lured by advertising. Almost <u>any</u> dealership will give you the <u>same</u> price as <u>any</u> so-called "sale" at any time of the year after you read this chapter (this excludes any manufacturer's rebates being offered).

THERE IS NO SUCH THING AS A CAR SALE.

You've seen advertisements with "Guaranteed $1,000 for your trade-in — drive it, tow it, just get it down here and get $1,000" or "free trip to Europe with every car purchase", etc. They just take this out of the profit margin of the selling price of the car. In other words, you get <u>less</u> of a discount when you try to wheel and deal. These "sale" advertisements are to get you to into the showroom, so they can close you on a new car and you will think you are getting a deal.

If you see special low interest rates on new car loans or leases, *be cautious*. This may only apply to a *portion* of the loan period. Read the fine print in the contract.

Don't fall for the biggest scam on the market — this is where the dealership advertises a big sale with a new low financing rate. They just do the classic "shuffle" — give smaller discounts to make up for the loss of profit in the low financing rates. **Many customers will happily pay $2,000 more for a car just to say they got 4.9% financing.** So instead of getting the $3,000 discount they would normally give, they only give you a $1,000 discount and take the rest of the profit margin to offset the low financing rate. To give you an example, a $10,000 car at 14% interest for 5 years is about $232 a month. An $11,000 car at 10% interest for 5 years is about $233 a month. See what I am getting at? What you save in one area, you pay for in another.

ANY LOW INTEREST RATE OFFERED FROM THE DEALERSHIP AND NOT THE MANUFACTURER IS USELESS.

However, there are two exceptions to this rule. The first is a secret sale from the manufacturer. The factory will offer special rebates or incentives to the dealer in order to sell more cars. With this added rebate, you can get a better deal — sometimes hundreds of dollars below dealer's invoice. You can assume there is a secret selling price if a car is very unpopular and the car lot is full of them.

The second is when the manufacturer offers a consumer rebate or reduced factory financing (not the dealer). This is when the manufacturer takes on approximately 50% (depending on the manufacturer) of the cost of the rebate financing costs. It will be advertised as "factory rebates or factory financing". However, many customers **still pay too much** because, preoccupied by the happiness of getting a low financing rate or rebate, they do not negotiate as hard as they should and end up paying more than necessary.

Watch out for cars that are advertised far too low. For example, a $16,000 car advertised for $9,999, even though the cost is $12,000. It's a great deal for the first person to get there. Everyone else gets "the switch". They are told that car is sold but the dealer has "one just like it right over here" (at almost full price). Remember, the dealer has only one shot at you. They believe that if you <u>do</u> <u>not</u> buy right then and there, you will not come back. **They will do or say almost anything to get you to buy today.**

Anti-lock brakes have commonly been portrayed by the salesman as the greatest safety invention since the bumper. Don't get over-sold. Although it is a *fantastic* safety feature, it can actually add to braking distance in certain situations (especially if you are a very good driver). You can also expect about a $600-$1,000 increase in the price for this one feature.

You may want to consider consulting injury, collision and theft rates on the particular cars you are interested in. These can affect your insurance rates dramatically. These statistics are available free from the Highway Loss Data Institute, 1005 North Glebe Rd., Arlington, VA 22201, (703) 247-1600.

One of the best ways to find the right car for you is to simply drive all of the models you are interested in. As corny as it sounds, after driving about five cars, you will know the one that is right for you. Don't be talked into buying a car on your first trip into a showroom.

A salesman's job is to make as much money as he can on each car. No matter how nice they are and whatever they might say, they are <u>not</u> on your side. Did you know a salesman can make over a **thousand dollars commission** selling a car if he does it right?! He makes approximately 20%-30% of the profit from the sale of the vehicle. He should be able to sell two to three cars a week. Let's say he only averages $500 commission per car — that's pretty good money (approx. $65,000 per year). The top sales people in the dealership easily clear $100,000 per year if they are really good. I bet you have no idea what kind of money these guys make if they are good at talking you into buying a new car. Don't think every salesman is rich; there are also many inexperienced ones making $20-30,000 per year.

There are two goals the salesman has in mind when he talks to you:

ONE IS TO GET YOU TO BUY A CAR TODAY – THE OTHER IS TO GET YOU TO PAY THOUSANDS MORE FOR THE CAR THAN YOU NEED TO PAY

So be prepared to use your poker face often and never, <u>never</u> reveal your hand, even after the deal is done.

The one exception to this situation is in a rural (small town) dealership. They are usually a less hectic atmosphere and have a reputation in the community. However, do not be fooled. They will still try to play games with you. Even my father paid $7,000 too much for a new Buick Park Avenue that he leased from a rural small town dealership (I guess he didn't read his son's book soon enough).

Be careful about what you wear when visiting the car dealer. You would be surprised how many times the price of a car rises when a salesman sees you walk in with an expensive jacket and gold rings. Dress well, but casually.

The first thing to remember is that...

IF THE SALESMAN DOESN'T KNOW HOW BADLY YOU WANT THE CAR, DON'T TELL HIM!

This gives you much more bargaining power.

Speaking of bargaining power; if you want a car that has to be ordered in, don't expect to bargain as low as one that is in stock. There are a couple of reasons for this. First, the sales manager wants the car to go towards the current month's sales targets (as the new car will probably not come in until next month). Secondly, they want to clear cars off the lot to make room for new, hotter selling models. Thirdly, it is a lot of hassle to order a car rather than selling one off the lot. Lastly, they don't want to take the risk of you having "buyers regret" and cancelling your order to buy a different model elsewhere.

Let's admit it, cash talks. If you are considering using your present car as a trade-in, don't reveal it. Dealers often give you less discount on a new car to make up for the handsome offer they've made on your old clunker. They can juggle numbers on your trade in to make it look as though you got a good deal. Play the game as though you are buying with a loan or cash. It simplifies your new car negotiation. In other words you want to get a rock bottom price on the car. Then reveal you want to trade your current car. Now you'll find the true price they will pay for it.

On that note, <u>don't</u> go into car shopping looking for a certain monthly payment. You will not get the car you want, but you will get a car that best suited the salesman's profit for that price range!

Never tell the salesperson what another dealer may have quoted you. He may try many tactics to do so, but just let him know that you will buy from the dealer that gives the best price and the overall best treatment.

Watch out for window sticker tricks. Many dealerships display a second sticker aside from the Manufacturer's retail selling invoice. It looks very official and is made to convey that the options are part of the car. This is an invoice with any extra accessories the <u>dealer</u> has installed (with <u>very</u> high profit margins) as well as various other charges (many of which are bogus). You will also see such things as protection packages, rustproofing, inland freight, dealer prep, A.D.P., etc. These are all very high profit extras the dealer loves to sell with the car. "A.D.P." or "M.V.A." is very official sounding,

BUT ALL IT MEANS IS ADDED DEALER PROFIT (ADP) OR MARKET VALUE ADJUSTMENT (MVA) – IN OTHER WORDS, A SHAM

Don't fall for Valuation Fee or Import Tariff. These are phony profit generators for the dealer.

Also beware of a "prep-fee". It could be $100 or more (depending on what the dealer thinks he can get away with). These are already calculated into the manufacturers sticker prices, **so don't pay for it twice.**

I recommend you deal with a "bottom line" approach. Although a dealer may initially give you a great deal on the car, maybe his extra fees make it much more expensive than down the street. Make sure you look at the total price. An agreed price of $14,000 may turn out to be $14,300 after the advertising fee has been added. Advertising fees can sometimes be negotiated down, if not completely eliminated, if you stand firm. This gives you reason to shop around as the dealer down the street may not charge this.

Look closely at invoices (dealer invoice and retail invoice). Some dealer invoices include the prep fee, advertising fee, or destination shipping charge. Make sure that you are aware of these prices and that the dealer doesn't charge you twice for it (once more on the retail invoice). **It happens often and is one of the most common rip-offs.** For example, if the dealer invoice does include a shipping charge, and the dealer agrees to give you a car at $200 over invoice, he may try to charge you this fee on top of the dealer invoice. It is pure profit for him.

If you sign over rebates to the dealer, in some states you won't have to pay sales tax on that amount. Make sure you know what you are signing.

It is not a smart idea to work one dealer's quote against another. It is not only time consuming and frustrating, but...

THERE IS A WAY TO DIRECTLY FIND OUT WHAT A GOOD PRICE IS IN SECONDS.

Here is the formula:

Factory Sticker Price minus 15% (12% on smaller cars) plus $600 = Your Target Price

This applies to most cars under $20,000 (markup increases with higher priced cars).

Actual market conditions can vary the price of your car. This formula is a good guideline for most dealerships and most cars. The price is based on supply and demand. But don't trust the salesman to tell you truly what is a hot seller.

This target price is the price which you should be willing to walk away from the deal for.

For more exact prices, you can also obtain a copy of *Edmunds Price Guides* at 515 Hempstead Turnpike, West Hempstead, NY 11552 or *Black Book New Car Invoice Guides* from National Auto Research, P.O. Box 758, Gainsville, GA 30503. They publish dealer car costs and their options at cost. It is an **invaluable** resource to have the exact dealer cost when bargaining with your salesman.

ONE OF THE MOST CLOSELY GUARDED SECRETS IS THAT THE DEALER GETS A 3% REBATE OF THE SELLING PRICE OF THE CAR LESS ABOUT $2/DAY OVERHEAD (RENTAL) FEE FROM THE MANUFACTURER.

So if the dealership sells a car at the dealer invoice price of $10,000, they will automatically get back $300 from the factory. This is why most dealers can sell a car just a little over their invoice cost!

It is estimated that more than 90% of car buyers pay too much for their cars. Sometimes more than $3,000 too much!

So now let's get into some of the really good stuff!

When is the best time to buy a car? Every dealership sets goals for the number of cars to be sold each month. If they have not reached these goals nearing the end of the month, they are more willing to bargain to attain themat the end of the month. It is difficult to get a good deal on a weekend. A salesman would rather spend his time with a naive, impulse-buying customer so that he can make lots of money, than with an educated car buyer that he would have to spend a lot of time on and not make much profit. Not as many people buy on weekdays, so the sales staff is hungrier for business. Another little pointer is to try to buy later in the day when the sales staff is tired. The secret is...

BUY ON THE SECOND LAST DAY OF THE MONTH AND GET AN EXTRA $400 DISCOUNT INSTANTLY!

They are so desperate to meet or beat their sales targets that they will drop $400 lower than on any other day! Keep in mind that this only works if the car is delivered on that or the next day (before the end of the month). If it is not, the car does not go on the current month's sales numbers. If it goes on that month's sales target, they may possibly reach a higher kickback bonus and the dealership doesn't have to pay interest (sometimes called a rental fee) on the car from the manufacturer. This is known as "floor planning". For big dealerships, this can get into the tens of thousands of dollars per month. If you want this discount, make it clear you want to pick up the car tomorrow.

Wondering when the best time of year to buy a car is? The answer is...**any time is fine!** You will realize there are never any true sales. They just mark the sticker price lower, but you can still negotiate to just over dealer cost on any day. The only exception to this is when a manufacturer sponsors a cash rebate or low financing - but keep in mind these should be subtracted from the negotiated price you would normally pay. This will make it so you are buying the car under dealer invoice cost. The dealer still makes money when the car is sold under invoice cost because the manufacturer takes the loss on the cash rebate or low financing, not the dealer.

Is buying a demonstrator a good deal? The salesmen are supposed to pamper these cars, but the reality of the matter is most of them drive them like maniacs because it is not their car. Many people are lured by a "big" discount on an almost new car. Generally, these cars are not such good deals because you can buy a brand new car for a little bit more than the price of the demo if you get the proper discount on the new car. For example, a new car might be $20,000 and the demo $16,000. Well, you could probably buy a brand new car for $16,500 when you negotiate using the skills and techniques shown in this chapter.

Another popular question is: **"Is buying last year's model worth the savings"?** Generally, yes, but not as much as you may think. Again, this is similar to the case with the demo car. The dealer makes a small discount look like a big discount. Keep in mind that the dealer will get a 5% rebate from the manufacturer when any old model car is sold.

Generally, the more you know about car buying, **the more you will save.** Again, keep in mind that it is the salesman's job to squeeze <u>every</u> last dollar out of you using any method possible. Don't be tricked by their smiles and friendly personalities. There are schools to teach them how to maximize profits on each car deal. They meet on a daily basis with their sales managers and attend seminars or courses on the art of selling.

As mentioned before, don't talk about trade-ins or your worry about the monthly payment because you'll get burned every time. Always discuss trade-ins, financing, etc. <u>after</u> a cash deal has been reached. But be ready. They will try to buy your trade-in for far below wholesale value. It is more troublesome, but try to sell your car privately. You will always get <u>much</u> more money for it.

You will notice that most salesmen have similar techniques when you are first approached. They will greet you, then build a rapport to gain your confidence and trust. They will then qualify you to see if you are a true "buyer", and finally seek out what "hot buttons" will motivate you to buy today. Examples of this are "What features are most important to you? Do you have a trade-in? Do you plan to finance and what is your budget? Describe your perfect car? If I can get you a great deal, will you be buying today"?

After a test drive, the salesman may say anything to make you commit so he can get you in the showroom where the deal is made.

IT IS HIS JOB TO SELL YOU A CAR <u>TODAY</u>, EVEN IF IT IS THE WRONG CAR FOR YOU.

His job is to convince you that whatever brand he is selling is the best brand for you and he has a perfect car in stock to suit your needs. He may talk to only two or three customers a day. If he doesn't sell you a car, he knows he will probably never see you again, so expect him to **say** or **do** anything to get you to buy **today**.

If you don't feel comfortable with a particular salesman, simply ask to deal with someone else. It may feel awkward, so a simple way to state this is "Please don't take this the wrong way; you seem like a nice gentleman, but for some reason I do not feel comfortable around you. Maybe our personalities clash, I'm not sure. Could I deal with another salesman? This is nothing against you personally".

He has a few secret principles he <u>must</u> abide by to "close" you. First he will always try to remain in control. He may be friendly and nice in the beginning, but as the deal gets closer, you will notice his voice may become more stern and controlled. The **more** in control he stays, the **more** money he can rake out of you. If he cannot accomplish this task, a "closer" or sales manager may step in, so be aware.

The next step in the salesman's procedure is to complicate the deal. The idea is to start talking trade-in values, rebates, and car prices all at one time to confuse the **true** selling price of the car. That is why it is so important to never mention a trade-in. He can make it look like you are getting a great deal on a car with an exaggerated trade-in value, but will over inflate the selling price to compensate.

He will also use time to close the deal for him. In essence, he will try to wear you down. If he cannot get you to buy at his price after 20-30 minutes, he may purposely stretch out the dealing process until you do. Thousands of people get impatient much too early and pay hundreds and sometimes thousands more for a car.

BE PREPARED TO SPEND 2 HOURS JUST BARGAINING FOR YOUR TERMS

When you consider that it can save you a thousand dollars, that isn't bad for a few hours work, right?

The following is a general guide on what the dealer should be allowed for profit. Keep in mind that this is not profit above the dealer's cost, but *total* profit. By that I mean that almost every car dealer is awarded 3% of the dealer's cost from the manufacturer for selling the car. So if you have a car that has a dealer cost of $10,000, the dealer will receive $300 back from the manufacturer. If an acceptable profit is $500, you should be paying only $200 over the dealer's invoice.

Dealers Invoice	Acceptable Profit
Up to $10,000	$ 500
10,000 - 15,000	$ 750
15,000 - 20,000	$1,000
20,000 - 25,000	$1,500
25,000 - 30,000	$1,750
30,000 - 35,000	$2,000
35,000 - 40,000	$2,250
40,000 - 50,000	$2,500
50,000 - 70,000	$3,000

For example, buying a $15,000 car at $200 over the invoice price really gives the dealer $650 in profit because of the 3% rebate he gets from the manufacturer.

All of these will depend on current market value. You will be surprised at how many dealers will sell for lower profits than listed above. Remember to **always** lowball the dealer, he may agree to a price much lower than what you expected if you are a persistent and a smart buyer.

Without referring to any price guides (like *Edmunds Price Guide*), the markup on base sticker prices is generally as follows:

10% on economy cars
12% on sub-compact
15% on compact cars
16% on sporty cars (e.g. Camaro)
18% on intermediates (e.g. Cutlass)
20% on smaller luxury cars (e.g. Grand Prix)
22% on full sized cars (e.g. Caprice)
25% on luxury cars (e.g. Cadillac)
20% on pickups and vans

Markup on options is as follows:

• 30% on appearance and convenience items (vinyl roof, air conditioning, etc.)

- 20% on performance items (transmission and suspension options)
- 50-100% on extended warranties
- 100-200% on rust proofing, upholstery protection, paint protection packages

This means that the more options you have on the car, the higher the markup; and the more room you have for negotiating.

Almost all car dealers have a minimum profit deal they have to obtain. This is usually $200 over invoice. There's are ways to buy $50 over invoice shown in my special reports.

There are many bargaining techniques that work well — we will go over a couple of them. The first is probably the most commonly-used method.

After a test drive, make an opening offer of about 4% lower than your target price. Anything lower and they will think your expectations are unreasonable and you are not a serious customer. You might say "If you can sell that car at $21,300, I'll take it today. Here's my credit card (or cheque) for deposit". This shows you are a serious buyer. They can actually **taste** a sale being made.

They may think they're in control with a credit card or deposit check, but you know you can walk away from the deal at **any point** with your deposit in hand. You can even walk away after the contract has been signed and your trade-in is locked up in their garage. **As long as you don't take the car with you, you can walk away and demand your trade-in back** (verify with your own state laws). Many people don't know that and get caught in a deal they don't want.

Never expect the salesman to accept your first offer. You now counter offer at the halfway point between your first offer and the target price. Remember to think in terms of negotiating up from your price, not down from the salesman price. Make sure the salesman checks with his manager after every offer, even if he says the manager will never approve it. Insist on this. The sales manager is the one who makes the final decision, **not the salesman.**

Gradually increase your price by $100 until you hit your target price. Make sure the last two increases are by $50, not $100. The salesman will feel as if you are getting close to giving up and walking out the door.

Once you have reached your target price, do not budge an inch. Mention you have checked around at car prices and their cost and will absolutely not pay more than that. You may even state "I am buying a car in the next few days, if not from you, from one of your competitors; the decision is completely up to you".

If the salesman will not accept your target price, increase one last time by $50 and state that this is your final offer, you refuse to pay more for the car! It is <u>important</u> that you put pressure on the salesman by threatening to leave if this last offer is not accepted.

He will definitely see the manager one last time. The majority of the time, he will return stating the manager needs $100 more to close the deal. This is used as a last resort to increase profits. Stand firm and repeat your last offer one more time. The majority of the time the dealer will finally give in to the price.

If the deal doesn't go through then, you can massage the sales-person's ego and remind him of his stake in the game. It may go something like this; "I really appreciate you spending all this time with me, I know you are doing your best. It would be a shame if your manager didn't approve this deal and you didn't make the commission. You really deserve it".

Many times you may have to walk toward the door to get them give into your deal. Remember to walk out the door slowly, give them a chance to chase you down and say "wait a minute". The manager restrains salespeople from giving in too early. You may even hear something like "sorry, that is our lowest price. If you cannot meet this price we will have to give your deposit back and sell the car to someone else". He will seem so sincere, but just wait him out and play the role that you are going to walk away.

REMEMBER, IT IS HIS JOB TO CONVINCE YOU THAT THE DISCOUNT YOU WANT IS IMPOSSIBLE.

Do not be afraid to walk out the door without your dream car — you can always come back. It is <u>necessary</u> to show the salesman that you are not fooling with your low offer.

If you are ever on your way out the door, and the salesperson says "wait a moment, let me check something for you, I'll be right back". He has "T.O.'d" you. This is where he has gone back to "Turn you Over" to the manager to see if he can close the deal. These managers are often paid well over $80,000 and are good at what they do, so be careful.

Car dealerships make a lot of their money in future servicing of that vehicle. Don't forget to remind the manager that you will be bringing the car back for service work. You might say, "you will be getting much more of my money over the years when I bring it back in for maintenance and repairs".

The best part is that you can play this game at as many car dealers as you want until you find the deal you like best. Just because you agreed on the price doesn't mean you have to commit to it right there.

You may be thinking, "must I play this haggling game"?

The answer is: only if you don't want to pay $500, $1,000 or even $2,000 or more for your car! More than 90% of car buyers do not play this game and pay far too much for their vehicles.

THOSE BUYERS DON'T HAVE THE INSIGHT GAINED FROM THIS BOOK!

There has been a recent trend among manufacturers to introduce no-haggle, one price dealerships. Cars are generally priced $300 -700 above invoice, depending on current market conditions. This is not the lowest price since the knowledge from this book will show you how to haggle a better deal down the street. But for people who don't feel comfortable haggling or just don't have the time for it, definitely look around for the "no-dicker sticker" dealers.

There are a few other ways that salesmen are trained to take your money.

First is the lie that there is "no discount". He might state such things as "there are discounts on last year's models, but there are never discounts on new models". Or the popular one at Japanese car dealerships; "these things are selling like hot cakes, we can't keep them in stock; there is no discount". They may insist on this a few times. When they are so sincere, it makes sense, doesn't it? Don't be fooled, there is <u>always</u> a discount.

DON'T BE CONNED INTO BELIEVING A SMALL DISCOUNT IS REALLY A BIG DISCOUNT.

This is one of the <u>best</u> weapons of the salesmen. If he can get you to believe that a $500 discount is unbelievably good, he can put hundreds of dollars of commission in his pocket because a $1500 discount was actually possible.

Women salespeople have been used very effectively in the showroom. They can charm and relax the customers. You would never think a woman would take advantage of you, they are so sweet and gentle, right? Think again, they are trained just like any other salesperson. Female customers generally feel more comfortable with a woman salesperson. But don't fall for the fellow sister act. They will take your money as fast as any other salesperson — sometimes even faster.

Speaking of women, female customers generally have the idea that import cars are much more reliable, and since they are often not as aware of the automotive industry as many male customers, they end up getting price-gouged by an import dealer and buying a car beyond their budget. A Harvard study showed that compared to white men, white women pay 40% higher markup and black women a 300% higher markup on new cars, so you women out there, be extra careful!

Once the price is settled, you begin to discuss financing and trade-ins. Remember, the dealer can really take advantage of you with high interest rates on financing and trade-in offers. If you have a good credit rating, do not hesitate to proclaim that and go to the bank for a better loan rate.

Keep in mind that you do not have to commit to the deal even if you have agreed upon a price. If you are not happy with the arrangements or want to think it over, just leave. They might try to state that the "special" price you were getting is only good for today. Don't buy into that line if they feed it to you! You can walk in a week later and buy the same car for the same price you agreed upon in an instant.

Don't fall for the "100% trade in" scam. This is where the dealer advertises he will give you 100% of your original purchase price as trade-in toward a new car. The catch is that it is the original purchase price less "necessary" repairs. These repairs are far from necessary and are charged at outrageous prices. Of course your car will need a new paint job at $2,000., etc. You would not believe the number of customers that leave very happily, claiming that they just got 100% of their original car's price back.

Back to your trade-in. As mentioned, do not bring it up until you have made a cash deal on the car. If you raise the issue of the trade-in too soon, you give the salesman two very powerful opportunities. He is trained to ask you many questions about your car to see how you feel about it. This is used to show him what approach he should take. One of the most popular approaches is for him to offer you much more than the car is worth. It just came out of the profit of the new car so you won't get as great a discount. But it is a hot button that might get you to buy today. If you thought your car was worth $500 and he offers you $1,000, you are mightily tempted to buy a car today. An opportunity like this may not come again, right? You may even think he is making a mistake and you better take advantage of it now. Don't be naive; it is all planned.

If you are emotionally attached to your current car, his second option is to slowly go over all the bad points of the car to diminish its value. Either way, the salesperson is again paid a commission on the difference between the trade-in's true value and the purchase price he has offered to you.

Depending on your state law, there can be a very large tax advantage when trading in a vehicle.

YOU WILL ONLY PAY THE TAX ON THE DIFFERENCE BETWEEN THE TRADE-IN VALUE AND THE NEW CAR PRICE!

For example, if you bought a $17,000 car, and the dealership gave you $7,000 for your old vehicle, you would only pay tax on $10,000, not $17,000. If your retail sales tax is 7%, tax paid on $17,000 is $1,190 and tax on $10,000 is $700. **You are $490 ahead**. In other words, if you were to sell your car privately, you would have to get a minimum of $7490 to equal the same deal at the dealership. This is due to the fact that you would not be using a trade-in vehicle anymore and would have to pay tax on the entire new car price. This may make up for the low offer the dealer has offered you on your old vehicle. Even though you should keep this in mind, you can generally sell your car privately for a much higher price than the dealer will ever offer (including the tax break).

There are six basic games the salesman will play, so let's go over them.

The first game is where he will give you discounts in one area to completely rip you off in another. For example, if the dealer has you sold on all the high profit margin items, like rustproofing, ADM and extended warranty, he might give you a great discount. Or he may offer you big bucks for your trade-in while giving only a small discount on your new car. In the end, he is still making enormous profit.

I will give you a perfect hidden example of this. You walk into the dealership to look at a new Corvette. You have a trade-in that is worth about $6,000. The salesman hasn't been able to sell you the car. Just as you are about to give up your dream car, the manager appears and asks the salesperson to find out who owns the red Oldsmobile Eighty Eight out front. You admit you are the owner. The manager goes on to tell you he has a customer who is dreaming of a red Eighty-Eight. He was willing to pay $9,000 for it. "If you want to sell your car, I will give you $8,000 for it just for the chance to get him back to buy it. I can't pay you cash, but I can give you $8,000 trade-in value towards anything on the lot. You'll never find a deal like this again. Eight thousand dollars and we will finance the rest".

Well, **no such customer exists**. He is giving you $2,000 extra for your car, but he will probably sell you that Vette at almost full price and still make a ton of money overall.

The second game is based on ego. The salesman uses your ego and self-image to get you to spend more money. They praise you for being so "decisive" when what they really are saying is that you're easy to manipulate and quick to give in. If you try to change your mind or tell them what you want, they will try to make you feel bad about it. For example, "You don't want the extended warranty? But you said before that having extra protection after your last car breaking down was really important, didn't you"?

The third is called the "difference game". This is where they attempt to make the deal confusing with trade-ins, options, rebates and discounts. They will not tell you the price of any of the separate items but give you a **different figure**. For example "I can send you home in this new car for the difference of $9,580".

The fourth game is a simple endurance game. The idea is to wear you down until you just sign because you are too tired to argue and sick of the hassle. He forces you to invest so much time that you are reluctant to let it go. You need to put the salesperson in the position where he is the one who wants to make a deal.

The fifth game is one of intimidation. The salesman will try to become a serious authority figure. We take a salesman's advice when buying a stereo or microwave and we also do the same with a car (even though we don't always realize it). He may say such things as "How dare you insult me, I have been working hard to get you a good deal, and you have the nerve to tell me it is not good enough". Most people would back down and say "sorry, I guess you are right to an extent". Just because he bought you a bag of chips and a pop doesn't mean you have to buy a $15,000 car from him. He may come out with "After all the time I spent with you showing you everything, you are going to go and buy a car from someone else? Is that how much you appreciate my time and effort"?

The last game is based on elements of trust between you and the salesman. He will do everything to convince you that this one time you have met an honest car salesman and do <u>everything</u> to gain your friendship and trust. A tell-tale sign is the good cop/bad cop routine. He plays the nice guy and blames everything on the manager. The manager doesn't mind because it raises profits.

Be polite and friendly when bargaining. You will not get a great deal if you insult the salesman (or car) or ramble on like an auctioneer. People, even salespeople, react to the way they are treated. It's human nature. If you try to play the "expert" he will try to prove you wrong. If you belittle him when negotiating, you'll only succeed in driving the price up.

One objective is to get the salesperson to devote a lot of energy and time to closing the sale. It gives you more bargaining power. After the salesman has invested this much time and can picture the deal done, it is harder to let the sale go. In other words, you can get a better price.

Many times you will find a car that you like that has many more options than you want. Most cars on the lot have added options for a reason... **that is where they make most of their money.**

Scale down the options you don't need. A sunroof can add $300-$1,000 to the price of a new car; all-wheel drive can add $1,000-$2,500; automatic transmission can add $500-$1,700. Also consider gas mileage. If you drive 15,000 miles per year at $1.20 per gallon, you could save $400 in gas expense by driving a sub-compact instead of a sports utility vehicle. Remember, it is the salesman's job to convince you these options are something you need.

There is usually only one way to get what you want...

BE FIRM!

In very blunt terms, you need to say, "Here's my money and here's what I want". You will get results. If you say you have "X" number of dollars to spend and you want "X" options, and you don't want the rest, they will find ways to accommodate you. If you are not firm, they will spend all day trying to tell you why the options on the car are so important and why you should spend the money on them.

Be prepared to walk away from the deal and leave them with your phone number if they change their mind. Remember, you can always come back — but I think you will find the salesman calling you within 24 hours telling you how he can work a deal to satisfy you. Some options may be removed or they may transfer a car from another dealership.

Most car dealers do not enjoy transferring a car from another dealership because it is a hassle and they will have to pay the other dealership at least $400 for the privilege of transferring the car (however, sometimes dealers can trade one of their vehicles for the other dealer's vehicle to make it an even trade, and therefore, free). This comes <u>directly</u> out of the profit margin and sometimes makes it tougher to get a great deal. If this situation happens, there is a sneaky trick you can pull. Once you see the salesperson coming to the office with the printout for the different dealer's inventory and where the car you want is, you can start asking him irrelevant questions in order to stall and get a glimpse at what dealership has the car you want. Then go there to get a better price directly.

Seriously re-consider ordering a car from the factory. Most dealerships will promise you two to three weeks, but expect around a two month wait. Also watch out for dealers trying to tell you he cannot discount the price because the car is specially ordered. **This is hogwash**. You can get the same discounts as for any car

car you would buy off the lot. Actually, the dealer makes more money on the same discount because with a special order car, he is not paying interest on the money he has borrowed to put the car on his lot.

Usually after you have agreed on a price and maybe even signed a sales contract, expect the manager and salesman to try to sell you extras you probably don't need. These such things are extended warranties, rustproofing, paint sealant and upholstery guard. These are almost a complete waste of money. Expect these items to be pushed really hard since they have not made as much profit on your deal as they would have liked.

THESE EXTRAS ARE ALMOST PURE PROFIT AND THEY WILL SAY JUST ABOUT ANYTHING TO SELL THEM.

On that note, do not be tricked into paying for extra items like rustproofing or fabric protection because it has been listed on the car's sales sticker as an option. If the manager says you have to buy one of these to get the deal you wanted, it is not too late to walk away from the whole deal.

Here are some interesting facts about the extras. Extended warranties are high profit items, and usually lousy investments. The salespeople make them sound like you would be a fool not to take it. **Don't fall into the trap.** If you ever do bring your car in for extended warranty work, you will usually find out that it is not covered, or "by the way — we found a few other problems that will cost you $300". If you absolutely insist on making the car dealer richer by buying an extended warranty (sometimes called a service contract), only purchase one that is underwritten by the vehicle's manufacturer. Never buy an warranty underwritten by insurance companies or individual dealerships; they are usually a bad bet. If they go bankrupt (which has happened often in the past), your warranty becomes *absolutely useless.*

Accident, health, life, and disability insurance are extremely expensive at the car dealership. Go to a local insurance agent and get much better coverage at a fraction of the cost.

Rustproofing and undercoating is another great sham. Most cars are rust treated at the factory. There is nothing additional needed. The dealership usually charges $300-$400 for the same service that you could get for $150 at any rustproof center (however, check that rustproofing by outside companies, does not void your corrosion warranty). Actually, some manufacturers (GM for example) have stated that additional rustproofing can create damage to the environment and also <u>reduce</u> the corrosion resistance of your vehicle. Other manufacturers have stated that any additional rust protection done by any company, including the dealership, <u>voids the corrosion warranty of your new car</u>.

Paint sealant is an absolute joke. A good can of wax is all your car will ever need. Upholstery guard you can do yourself for about $20. Buy two cans of Scotchguard at your local auto parts store and spray it on. It makes liquid bead on the surface without soaking in (as long as pressure is not applied).

Processing fees are "icing on the cake". They can range from $100-$200. This is a completely bogus fee; added profit for the dealer. It is usually on the sales contract just below the price of the car. Cross this fee off the contract! If the salesman or manager questions you, nicely tell him that you are not paying any extra fees and you are willing to buy your car elsewhere if it stays there. They will not throw a deal away over a $100 fee.

Don't be afraid to ask for a photocopy of the contract to take home and read before you sign. There is so much legal jargon, it is difficult to understand and sort out with the pressure of a salesman waiting for you and tapping his fingers on the dotted line.

MOST NEW CAR CONTRACTS LEAVE PLENTY OF LEEWAY FOR THE DEALER TO CHANGE THE DEAL AFTER IT IS SIGNED!

So be careful what you are signing. Many contracts state a 20% penalty for cancelling the contract. <u>Make</u> <u>sure</u> you don't sign a contract that has more than a 2% penalty fee. Also <u>make</u> <u>sure</u> there is a specific delivery date for the car, not "as soon as possible", and make sure it is stated that you have the right to cancel the contract if that delivery date is not met.

Remember the days when you got a great deal on items because you paid cash? Well, things have changed. Some people come into a car dealership thinking they will get a better price if they pay cash. Much of the dealer's profit comes from financing (or should I say financing rip-offs)? This is where, after you have negotiated a good deal and are worn out and exhausted, the finance officer tries to slip by some high interest rates or bogus financing charges. Don't let your guard down yet. These people are paid to make money from you. You may question whether their interest rates are good and the reply will always be "Of course, we compete with any bank. Don't you think when GM or Ford borrows billions of dollars, they get a better rate than you would? They are passing that savings along to you". It make sense. But it is his job to try and get 12-15% from you even if the going rate is 10%.

THIS CAN INSTANTLY ADD $1,000 OR MORE PROFIT FOR THE CAR DEALER

If you have driven a hard bargain, be prepared to get your financing outside the dealership. If you decide to finance it at the dealership, you will pay something extra for that convenience; a percentage point or two of interest or perhaps a fee of some sort.

Make sure you take delivery of the car during daylight hours. You can examine the paint job and body for scratches and dents. Drive the car around the lot to make sure everything is OK. Do not take delivery of the car if there are any serious cosmetic problems or if the car doesn't feel right. Remember, **the deal is not done until you pick up the car.**

If something is drastically wrong with the car after driving it around for a while, the courts have allowed people to return their cars for full refund within a couple of days.

As explained in chapter 1, if you cannot get results with a dealer you are having a problem with, see the zone manager. The zone manager knows the business can be crooked — he can't do anything about that. His job is to see the cheating is done subtly. If you complain to the zone manager, the dealer begins to sweat as the zone manager can make his business transactions with the factory living hell. The dealership will not risk that over a few hundred dollars.

You are probably wondering, if the car business is so crooked, why doesn't everyone know about it? The answer is simple. If you have been taken by a dealership, you will most likely deny it. It is humiliating to admit you have lost out and that others have won. The other reason is that most dealerships believe the best way to make money is to convince these people into thinking they got a great deal when they are <u>grossly overcharging them</u>.

One of the strongest points I can make is to be logical, wise, and...

DON'T LET YOUR EMOTIONS CONTROL YOU!

Trying to stay emotionally detached from the car you're falling in love with is very difficult. The salesman is <u>counting</u> on that love to give him the edge and let him take advantage of you.

Most of all, **use the knowledge found in this book to make the best decision for the particular situation that you are in**. But definitely do not tell them you have read this book. They do not want you to know what goes on.

GOVERNMENT AGENCIES AND CONSUMER GROUPS

American Automobile Association
1000 AAA Drive
Heathrow, FL 32746
(800) 477-6583 or (407) 444-7740
AAA provides services to members and operates mediation programs for members and dealers.

Better Business Bureau
Check local phone book for address
Provides reports and consumer information on dealers. Also operates a mediation program for complaints with dealers.

Center for Auto Safety
2001 S. Street NW
Washington, DC 20009
(202) 328-7700
A non-profit organization that lobbies on behalf of the consumer's interests in vehicle safety and quality. Also provides information on lemon laws and operates a lawyer referral service.

Chrysler Corp.'s National Owner Relations Department
P.O. Box 1086
Detroit, MI 48288
(800) 922-1997
Handles complaints not resolved at the zone managers level

Environmental Protection Agency
401 M Street SW
Washington, DC 20460
(202) 260-2090
Enforces all emissions control regulations and publishes an EPA gas mileage guide for all makes and model of automobiles.

Federal Trade Commission
6th and Pennsylvania Ave NW
Washington, DC 20580
(202) 326-2222
Has regional offices in major cities. Provides information on mediation and consumer complaints.

Ford Consumer Appeals Board
P.O. Box 5120
Southfield. MI 48086
Provides information on arbitration with Ford.

General Motors Product Service Publications
(800) 551-4123
Leave your name and address on the voice mail to be sent technical bulletins (mentioned in chapter 1) that might apply to your car.

National Automobile Dealers Association - AUTOCAP
8400 Westpark Drive
McLean, VA 22102
(703) 821-7000
Refers you to a local board that will answer questions on the AUTOCAP arbitration system and tells you if your dealer is a member.

National Highway Traffic Safety Administration
400 7th Street SW
Washington, DC 20590
(202) 366-9550
Reports safety defects and enforces safety regulations. Call 1-800-424-9393 to report safety problems or get information on safety recalls.

National Insurance Consumers Organization (NICO)
121 N. Payne Street
Alexandria, VA 22314
(703) 549-8050
Educates consumers on insurance issues and lobbies on behalf of consumer interests.

U.S. Department of Justice
Office of Litigation
P.O. Box 386
Washington, DC 20044
(202) 514-6786
Enforces federal laws covering price labeling of new cars.

HOW AND WHERE TO BUY A USED CAR (AND AVOID LEMONS)

If you haven't read the last chapter on buying a new car, read it! Much of the information there applies to buying a used car as well as to a new one.

Buying used can be very beneficial, especially if you're buying a higher priced vehicle. Most cars will depreciate 25% right after you drive them off the lot...

A CAR CAN DEPRECIATE
BY AS MUCH AS 40% IN TWO YEARS

Buying used can provide a great opportunity for you to save a lot of money.

For example, I prefer to purchase a car that is 2 years old. Many people can afford to buy a two year old BMW, but not a new one. They can now drive a car that is normally out of their price range and enjoy the prestige and excitement of a luxury car by buying used. Let someone else "eat" the depreciation for the first year or two since that represents the majority of it.

To determine the value of a used car, you can use a couple of methods. One is to look at the common price of similar vehicles in your area through the classified ads or local AutoTrader.

There are also publications you can refer to get retail and whole-sale values for most vehicles.

Blue Book - NADA used car guide
National Automobile Dealers Assoc.
8400 Westpark Dr.
McLean, VA 22102
(703) 821-7000
(800) 544-6232

Black Book
PO Box 758
Gainesville, GA 30503
(404) 532-4111
Used most commonly by banks and car dealers; generally lower values than the NADA guide.

Cars of Particular Interest (CPI)
PO Box 11409
Baltimore, MD 21239
Published price guide of postwar collectibles and special interest cars.

Most local bankers or car dealers carry the *Black Book*. If you have a friend in the business, you may be able to persuade them to let you keep a past issue of the book. This is a very inexpensive way to obtain the current wholesale value of vehicles you are interested in. Otherwise you will have to subscribe to the publication for about $70 a year.

Basically, there are three sources you can buy from: private individual, licensed car dealers (new or used) or at an auction.

Be wary of auctions. You never know what the car has been through, and once you buy it, you own it. If you do decide to buy a car at an auction, let me give you one important piece of advice. Don't wait until the bidding has cooled down to enter the contest. Many people think by entering late in the game, they have the edge. This is <u>not</u> the case. Anyone who enters the bidding this late is likely to stir the curiosity of others and unwittingly encourage them to join in. Many times cars would have been sold at a <u>fraction</u> of their value if it wasn't for the bidding being revived by people entering the bidding in the cool down stages.

Whether you buy from a dealer or a private individual, there are a few things to remember. Don't be overwhelmed by a car that is shiny and glossy. The <u>mechanics</u> of the car are what you should be concerned about. Don't buy a car because you feel you can trust the person that is selling it — some people simply don't know how to care for a vehicle.

If you are buying from a dealer, expect the same treatment as explained in the previous chapter when buying a new car. They may be a wonderful husband to their wife and a great father to their kids — the selling game is separate from the rest of life. **So beware!**

You may hear lines like "this is the best example I've seen in a long time" or "two other people are seriously interested" or "my brother wants to buy it if I don't sell it today" and so on.

If you decide to buy your used car from a dealer, a new car dealership is a good place to start. You won't find a great bargain here, but you will find cars that are solid. Most used cars sold from a new car dealership are trade-ins from their clients, and the dealership usually has background information on them. Cars they do not feel are good are usually sold to used car dealers down the street or sent to the auction.

GENERALLY, USED CAR DEALERS DON'T SEEM TO KNOW MUCH ABOUT CARS, BUT THEY SURE KNOW HOW TO MAKE THEM SHINE AND SELL THEM FAST!

Since this is where the main dealers get rid of the "unwanteds", your chances of getting a lemon are increased. However, the advantage to buying from a dealer rather than a private owner is that some cars can be purchased with a warranty which offsets some of the risk.

There is also a chance with a used car dealer that you are buying a former rental car. These cars are originally sold back to the car manufacturers or dealers and frequently found at auctions where the used car dealers buy them. If the salesman is reluctant to let you look at the odometer statement or ownership papers, find another car.

Many car dealers sell their vehicles in "as is" condition without any warranty. However, some states (Connecticut, Kansas, Maine, Maryland, Massachusetts, Mississippi, New York, Rhode Island, Vermont, West Virginia, and the district of Columbia) require dealers to sell their cars with warranties. The "warranty of merchantability" is the most common.

This means the seller promises that the product will do what it is supposed to. For example, a toaster will toast and a car will run. Another type of warranty is "warranty of fitness for a particular purpose". For example, if a dealer suggests you buy a certain vehicle for pulling a trailer, in effect, that vehicle should be suitable for hauling a trailer. Most warranties are "limited". This means you have to pay a portion of the repair. On the Buyer's Guide posted in all used car vehicles from a used car dealer will be the following information regarding warranty:

1. The percentage the dealer will pay for warranty work.
2. What exactly is covered.
3. The duration of the warranty.
4. Whether deductible applies.

Watch out for the difference between a warranty the dealer is offering and an unexpired warranty from the car manufacturer. Do they overlap? Also, make <u>sure</u> the manufacturer's warranty is transferable. This applies especially to people buying from a private seller. Most of us just assume the warranty is still in effect for a new owner. Many times you have to pay a transfer fee of $100 or more to the manufacturer.

Although you know my opinion of service contracts and extended warranties with new cars, sometimes these can be beneficial for used cars because the probability of breakdown is much greater. However, watch for the following things:

1. Does the manufacturer's warranty overlap the service contract?
2. Does the service contract extend longer than you plan to keep the car? If so, is it transferable or is a shorter one available?
3. What does it cover? Many claim "bumper to bumper" coverage, but read the fine print, **almost none of them live up to that!**
4. Is there a deductible required?

5. Does it cover towing and car rental while yours in being repaired?
6. Does it include routine maintenance such as oil changes and brake work?
7. Is there a cancellation or refund policy?
8. Who is legally responsible for fulfilling the terms of the warranty? Are they reputable?
9. Does it cover you if you move?
10. Do you pay first and then get reimbursed, or does it cover payments needed.

And most of all, keep in mind that a good looking car that comes with a warranty does not necessarily run well.

You can usually find a better deal buying from a private owner. However, one down side to buying privately is that some owners have a sentimental or emotional attachment to their car and think it is worth more than it really is. Many cars will appear to be worth less, but that is solely because they are not cleaned and prepared like those offers by dealers. This normally works to your benefit. Another down side is that you may be stuck with repair bills to fix problems you didn't find until after your purchase (this can happen with dealers too).

There are ways to avoid these expenses. One is to buy your car certified (or "safetied" as it is called in some states). This will avoid many of the obvious problems. You can also hire a mechanic to give the car you're interested in a vehicle inspection. It may cost you $50...

BUT CONSIDER IT AN INSURANCE POLICY SO YOU DON'T GET STUCK WITH A LEMON.

There is such a demand for this that most large cities have businesses that offer a mobile vehicle inspection service. They will come right to the prospective seller's house to inspect it.

Make sure the mechanic checks for the following:

1. Loose or worn belts

2. Worn or leaking hoses
3. Radiator and cooling system pressure test
4. Engine cracks or leaks
5. Timing and ignition system
6. Compression
7. Carburetor or injection system
8. PCV valve and accompanying system
9. Exhaust system
10. Clutch pedal free play
11. Oil level and condition (transmission too)
12. Battery and alternator output
13. Brake cylinder fluid levels and leaks
14. Starter
15. Water pump
16. Fuel pump
17. Voltage regulator
18. Axle damage or leaks
19. Drive shaft and U-joints
20. Transmission leaks
21. Shock absorber leaks
22. Ball joint play
23. Steering play
24. Brake system leaks
25. Brake linings and pads
26. Under body rust
27. Tires that indicate bad wheel alignment

As mentioned before, make sure all warranties outstanding are transferable and check if there is a cost associated with this.

One of the biggest dangers with buying privately is that you might encounter **a part time car dealer posing as a private seller.** These are people who buy cheap cars in their spare time and do everything to make them look great. They expend the least amount of money to make the vehicle look great. These cars are often the worst to purchase, they may have had their odometers tampered with or have major faults cleverly concealed. Some buy cars that have been "written off" from insurance companies after an accident and then rebuilt and sold as a good-looking car.

HERE ARE A FEW HINTS TO HELP YOU SPOT THESE ROGUES.

They will use "glamour" words in their advertisements, like "fabulous buy, very clean car, beautiful automobile" etc. When you phone and state you are calling about the "car for sale" (don't mention the make or model), they will ask "which car" if they repair or sell cars on the side (this is a _real_ giveaway). Insist on seeing the registration documents. Some of the part-timers still have the registration in the original owner's name and will come up with some excuse why it is like that. **Don't fall for it.**

Other things to look for with any used car is to see if all the physical specifications match on the registration documents. If the car says it is a red V-6 and it is a blue L-6, look for an engine replacement and a paint job following an accident.

The reason why I am going over all of this is one simple fact:

ONE OUT OF EVERY FOUR VEHICLES SOLD "USED" WAS EITHER REPORTED STOLEN, WAS AN ACCIDENT WRITE-OFF, OR HAD OUTSTANDING FINANCING AGAINST IT.

To give you a possible scenario: If you buy a car that has a lien against it (outstanding financing), _you_ are now responsible for the loan held against the car. The car could be repossessed since it really belongs to the finance holder. It is a simple way to lose the total purchase price of the car in one easy shot. If you paid $10,000 for the car, **you just threw away your hard-earned $10,000 in one big mistake.**

In some states/provinces you can purchase a report from the DMV listing the history of a car including its previous owners. It usually costs somewhere between $10-$25 — a very good investment!

When buying from the newspaper or Autotrader, the best time to get a good deal is while the ink on the ad is still wet. The next best is a couple of weeks later, by which time the seller is more apt to accept a lower price.

A few of things you will want to ask the owner over the phone: year and model, color, condition of engine/interior/bodywork, presence of rust how much oil the engine uses, how long the seller has owned the car, why he is selling it, and is the full service history available?

<u>Half</u> the cars will be in much worse condition than described.

When inspecting a car, don't walk around the car and gaze at it. Bring the proper clothes and tools to get right under the car. The car may have a rust free body and a beautiful paint job but...

YOU SHOULD CONCERN YOURSELF
WITH WHAT IS UNDERNEATH THE CAR!

These are where the big problems are found, the ones that cost you major dollars to repair.

Make sure you can take the car where you can give it a good workout...on bumpy roads...in stop and go traffic...and on a highway.

Watch out for owners that have a small problem with their car and claim it can be fixed really cheap. Take, for example, a car that grinds a little when shifting gears. The owner claims it is a simple problem to solve and will only cost $40 at a mechanic's garage. Try to remember that his grandma <u>really</u> <u>didn't</u> just drive it to church on Sunday. He may have a serious problem that could end up costing <u>you</u> hundreds of dollars to repair.

If a situation like this arises and you are determined to have that specific car, I strongly recommend you use the following approach. This is what you could say to the owner. "Well, I like the car and will take it, but before I take ownership of it and we handle the financial arrangements, let's take it to your mechanic to have that $40 part installed to repair the grinding noise. We will add the $40 to the price of the car, OK"?

If he is reluctant to do this, he probably knows a bigger problem exists. By using this method you protect yourself. Don't lay out a penny until you have gone with the owner to the mechanic's garage to fix the so-called "simple problem".

Now, let's talk price.

When you make an offer, it should be rejected by the owner (or dealer).

IF HE ACCEPTS YOUR FIRST OFFER, YOU ARE PAYING TOO MUCH.

Start low and be prepared to walk away. You are in the driver's seat; you can always turn around and come back and agree to the last price that he counter offered.

Expect to pay a higher price for a Honda, Toyota, or German car, they have a tendency to hold their value.

If you want to find out if the car you are considering has been recalled by the manufacturer for a safety repair, call 1-800-424-9393. Give them the Vehicle Identification Number, make, model and year.

Remember that a car with fancy lettering on the back, like GTS, will always cost you an arm and a leg in insurance. It is a factor you might want to consider. On that note, make sure the car is **truly** that model. They may have the emblem pronouncing it as a GTS model, but does the performance of the vehicle and registration match? This is a classic ploy for getting higher selling prices for a car.

If you buy a car that is 10 years or older (and especially if you are young), you may be able to buy classic car insurance. It has a much lower premium, but will also have a mileage restriction.

And now for the scary side of buying a used car. Did you know that The National Highway Traffic Safety Commission estimates that...

20% OF ALL PRIVATE VEHICLES AND 70% OF ALL FLEET VEHICLES HAVE HAD THEIR ODOMETERS ROLLED BACK.

You want to be able to spot an odometer that has been tampered with. I heard of a guy that spent the entire afternoon underneath his car with a drill, **winding thousands of miles away**. Look at the brake and gas pedals. Are they new? If so, they may be trying to hide wear and tear. Look for scratches on the numbers of the odometer as if from a small screwdriver. Fingerprints on the odometer inside the glass are pretty conclusive. Look at service records and check mileage readings on them. If there aren't any records, assume the worst.

And, of course, there is the large problem of cars "totaled" by drivers, bought from the insurance companies, rebuilt (often improperly and unsafely) and then resold. The seller can make **thousands per car**, but these cars can mean many problems for you. That is why a mechanic's inspection is so critical, you can find out if your car is a salvaged vehicle. There are lots of them around **so beware**.

Also look for typeovers, spelling mistakes or water marks on the registration. All could indicate forgery.

If you want to buy a car wholesale (without a dealer's license) some smaller dealers will take you to the auction with them for a fee (usually $200-$600 to buy the car of your choice). Keep in mind that these cars are usually cars other dealers didn't want and you are buying without test driving. Unless the car is a completely unsafe disaster, you cannot get any of your money back.

THE TRUTH ABOUT GOVERNMENT SURPLUS AND SEIZURE AUCTIONS

You may have seen the ads in magazines stating "Porsches $200, Corvettes $150". They then try to sell you a $20-$30 package on how to do it through government auctions. These advertisements claim that the Drug Enforcement Agency, Customs, and other government agencies sell these cars at auctions for whatever they can get for them. If these seem a little too good to be true, <u>you</u> <u>are</u> <u>right</u>, they are! Yet they aren't really lying either. Many years ago when no one knew about these auctions, you would see everything from luxurious cars to used mail trucks going through the auction at far below wholesale value. Once in a while a really beaten up car would cross the block and no one would want it so it would be sold for a <u>ridiculous</u> price like a few hundred dollars.

In the last few years a few people have exploited these auctions. Now too many people attend and push the prices back up to about 80% of retail levels. In other words...

YOU WILL ALMOST NEVER GET ANY DEAL AT A GOVERNMENT AUCTION!

Also, most cars that have been seized have been stored for extended periods of time. The government doesn't own them until all the trials have ended and the suspect has been convicted. This can sometimes take years. **Generally the cars are in very rough shape and almost all of them do not have ignition keys.**

All sales are final. If it falls apart in two days or has a blown engine when you buy it, **TOO BAD.**

You will have to arrange to have the car towed away a few days after the auction. Keep in mind once you get a new ignition, the car is not guaranteed to run. <u>Never</u> pay more than 1/2 the blue book value, 1/3 is even safer. This way you will still come out ahead if major repairs are necessary.

Your time is much better spent buying from other sources.

There is <u>one</u> exception. Buying from auctions held by your local county or city governments can prove profitable, since participating bidders are minimal and the prices can be low. Contact the local sheriff's office or fire department for information on how to purchase confiscated and surplus vehicles.